T0329390

Modernising Traditions and Traditionalising Modernity in Africa:
Chieftaincy and Democracy in Cameroon & Botswana

Francis B. Nyamnjoh

Langaa Research & Publishing CIG
Mankon, Bamenda

Publisher:

Langaa RPCIG

Langaa Research & Publishing Common Initiative Group

P.O. Box 902 Mankon

Bamenda

North West Region

Cameroon

Langaagrp@gmail.com

www.langaa-rpcig.net

Distributed in and outside N. America by African Books Collective

orders@africanbookscollective.com

www.africanbookscollective.com

ISBN: 9956-762-07-5

Table of Contents

Acknowledgements

I am grateful to the Wenner-Gren Foundation for Anthropological Research for funding my research on Cameroon, and to the Research and Publications Committee of the Faculty of Social Sciences at the University of Botswana, for funds to research chieftaincy in Botswana. An earlier version of this study was published under a different title in *The Dynamics of Power and the Rule of Law: Essays on Africa and Beyond* (2003), edited by Wim van Binsbergen in collaboration with Riekje Pelgrim. I am grateful to them for comments and editorial assistance. I am equally grateful to Henning Melber, who guest-edited a special issue *of Journal of Contemporary African Studies* (vol.21(2), 2003), in which an earlier version of the section on Botswana was published, as well as to participants at the July 2004 University of Durham, UK, conference on 'Traditional Accountability and Modern Governance in Africa', where an earlier version of this study was presented as a keynote with the title: '"Our Traditions are Modern, Our modernities traditional": Chieftaincy and Democracy in Contemporary Africa' I am grateful to Petr Skalnik and two anonymous reviewers for the journal *Modern Africa: Politics, History and Society*, who suggested useful revisions for the version of the study published in the journal (vol.2(2), 2014), and to the Stellenbosch Institute for Advanced Studies (STIAS) for a fellowship (April – June 2015) that enabled me to undertake the revisions. I am most grateful, especially, to all the chiefdoms and kingdoms where I have lived and/or studies through the years, for inspiring my social scientific curiosities.

Chapter 1

Chieftaincy Studies in Africa: An Overview

As I have argued elsewhere (Nyamnjoh 2005), it is commonplace to claim that liberal democracy and Africa are not good bedfellows, and how apt! Implementing liberal democracy in Africa has been like trying to force onto the body of a full-figured person, rich in all the cultural indicators of health Africans are familiar with, a dress made to fit the slim, de-fleshed Hollywood consumer model of a Barbie doll-type entertainment icon. But instead of blaming the tiny dress or its designer, the tradition has been to fault the popular body or the popular ideal of beauty, for emphasizing too much bulk, for parading the wrong sizes, for just not being the right thing. Not often is the experience and expertise of the designer or dressmaker questioned, nor his/her audacity to assume that the parochial cultural palates that inform his/her peculiar sense of beauty should play God in the lives of regions and cultures where different criteria of beauty and the good life come from. This insensitivity is akin to the behaviour of a Lilliputian undertaker who would rather trim a corpse than expand his/her coffin to accommodate a man-mountain, or a carpenter whose only tool is a huge hammer and to whom every problem is a nail. The historical difficulty of implementing liberal democracy in Africa attests to this clash of values and attempts to ignore African cultural realities that might well have enriched and domesticated liberal democracy towards a greater relevance. This call for domestication must however not be confused with the ploy by opportunistic dictatorships that have often hidden behind nebulous claims of African specificities to orchestrate highhandedness and intolerance.

Theorizing democracy and accountability in Africa ought to emphasise networking and creative domestication of encounters with others. This focus should check the application of misleading labels, and draw attention to the various pressures exerted on the state and private corporate entities by various groups in various ways for various reasons of empowerment. As people increasingly distrust states, markets and NGOs to accommodate their needs, they will continue to explore other avenues of fulfilling their expectations. In certain cases and situations functions usually served by civil society as *voluntary* organisations have been performed by *non-voluntary* groups and lobbies such as ethnic elite associations and development unions, often under *unelected* leadership (Nyamnjoh & Rowlands 1998; Fokwang 2009; Konings 2009; Mercer, Page & Evans 2009; Comaroff & Comaroff 2009). Walking the corridors of power and resources seeking political and economic empowerment and representation for their regions or peoples as cultural units, such ethnic associations or their representatives have often been more active and fruitful in the name of ordinary citizens and subjects than most formal voluntary associations in many an African country. The platinum-rich Bafokeng Tswana nation of the North West province, known as the 'Royal Bafokeng Nation', with kings who brand themselves as CEOs of 'Bafokeng, Inc.' – to cite one example only – just might have some lessons on creative improvisation and adaptation with changing circumstances that belie sweeping assumptions about the supposedly inherent fixation with the past and autocracy of systems of governance inspired by endogenous philosophies of personhood and leadership (Comaroff & Comaroff 2009: 98–116; Cook &

2

Hardin 2013; Manson 2013). If chiefs are individuals with agency like every other individual in society, there is nothing inherently dictatorial about them as people or chieftaincy as an institution, just as there is nothing inherently democratic about presidents as people or the institution of the state (Fokwang 2009; Nyamnjoh 2003). Far from distinguishing in abstraction between elected and unelected authorities, Afrobarometer survey reports indicate that Africans who live under so-called traditional authority and democratic governance 'do not draw as sharp a distinction between hereditary chiefs and elected local government officials as most analysts would expect' (Logan 2009: 101; Logan 2013; Fanthorpe 2005). Indeed, as Fo Angwafo III demonstrates in his autobiography – *Royalty and Politics: The Story of My Life* (Angwafo III, 2009) – one person can straddle both the hereditary and elected offices with fascinating ambiguity that challenges us as scholars to rethink conventional categories and concepts.

No institution illustrates this accommodation of influences better than chieftaincy, which unfortunately is often wrongly reduced by scholars to the chief as an individual and credited with far more might than right, and with a frozen idea of tradition. We throw the baby out with the bathwater whenever in our scholarship we are keener to prescribe and transform than to understand the chiefs and chieftaincy we so desperately want out of the African accountability equation. Yet the more we scrutinise purportedly incompatible rituals of verification and accountability without misleading dichotomisations (e.g. 'traditional'/'modern', 'irrational'/'rational', 'African'/'Western', 'elected'/'unelected'), the more negotiability, interconnectedness, nuances, symmetries and conviviality inform the realities we seek to keep asunder (Kelsall 2003; Angwafo III, 2009; Comaroff & Comaroff 2009: 98–116).

Reality is often much more than meets the senses, and thus requires appreciation at different levels, including the apparent and the subtle, the physical and the metaphysical (Mbembe 2001:142-172; Moore and Sanders 2001; Nyamnjoh 2001a, 2012).

In Africa, chieftaincy is a dynamic institution with pre-colonial roots in some cases, and largely colonial and post-colonial origins in others (Harneit-Sievers 1998; Geschiere 1993; Valsecchi 2007; Cheka 2008; LiPuma & Koelble 2009; Makahamadze, Grand & Tavuyanago 2009; Knierzinger 2011; Dean 2013; Omagu 2013; Goodfellow & Lindemann 2013; Machacek 2013; Ajaegbo 2014; Chakunda & Chikerema 2014; Mawere & Mayekiso 2014; Chigudu 2015). Prominent among the approaches in chieftaincy studies have been what I qualify as partial theories rose to meta-narratives of expectation of the expiring of traditional societies, institutions and cultures. Modernisation theorists for instance have, in tune with their evolutionary and homogenising perspectives, expected such expirations as the natural course of things. Dependency, or revolutionary, theorists on the other hand have been critical of all traditional institutions, chieftaincy in particular, for having been appropriated or created by colonial, apartheid and post-colonial states for various purposes, including repression and the creation of the division between 'citizens' and 'subjects' (Mamdani 1996). Both partial theories have largely regarded chieftaincy as more 'might' than 'right', and have consequently wished for chieftaincy to be abolished or ignored, in order to make room for citizenship based on the individual as an autonomous and accountable agent. These theoretical approaches are prescriptively modernist (*à l'occidentale*) in their insensitivity to the cultural structures of African societies, and to the domesticated agency of Africans.

4

The future of accountability they envisage for the continent has little room for institutions and traditions *assumed* to be primitive, repressive and unchanging in character. Chieftaincy, these theories suggest, will always look to the past or to the state for inspiration in the service of exploitation and of marginalisation by high-handedness. Within these frameworks, chieftaincy is seldom credited with the ability to liberate or to work in tune with popular expectations, even when such expectations are largely unaccounted for by such competing rhetoric's as liberalism and socialism. As John Comaroff has rightly observed, the tendency in these partial theories to focus analysis 'almost exclusively upon institutional and constitutional arrangements', assumes 'the classical dichotomy between ascription and achievement' and 'takes as given that stated rules should actually determine the careers of actors in the public arena' (Comaroff 1978: 1). The tendency has also been to reduce chieftaincy to chiefs, to freeze chiefs in traditions portrayed essentially as incompatible with individual agency, and to assume from the presumed failings of chiefs the failings of chieftaincy as a socio-cultural and political system. The tendency is to argue oblivious of the fact that institutions and individuals mutually constitute one another, at different points in history, depending on the relationships we choose to privilege. It is true that the body of literature less categorical about dichotomies between ascription and achievement is growing. However, the tendency, even in such apparently accommodating literature, remains one of tolerating an African exception to a Eurocentric index of what democratic leadership ought to be. It is couched in terms of how to adapt or harness traditional or hereditary leadership in promoting democratic values, as if the very idea of democracy is at odds with a system of authority where leaders do not appear to have been chosen by popular ballot through an election of some kind (Cheka 2008; LiPuma & Koelble 2009; Makahamadze, Grand & Tavuyanago 2009; Dean 2013; Omagu 2013; Goodfellow & Lindemann 2013; Machacek 2013; Ajaegbo 2014; Chakunda & Chikerema 2014; Mawere & Mayekiso 2014; Chigudu 2015).

During the euphoric 1950s and 1960s, when 'expectations of modernity' were rife (Ferguson 1999), modernisation theorists predicted that chiefs and chieftaincy as agents and institutions of representation and accountability, would soon become outmoded, and be replaced by 'modern' bureaucratic offices and institutions (Warnier 1993: 318; Harneit-Sievers 1998: 57, Mappa 1998). Even underdevelopment, dependency and socialist theorists did not seem to give chieftaincy much of a chance (Harneit-Sievers 1998: 57-60), as they regarded them as lacking in the ability to mobilise social and political change. This view has not entirely disappeared, as some theorists continue to argue for a common political and legal regime that guarantees equal citizenship for all, and for the abolition of the 'decentralised despotism' that informs bifurcations like 'citizens' and 'subjects' (Mamdani 1996; Maloka 1995, 1996; Hendricks & Ntsebeza 1999). At present however, scholars increasingly acknowledge the resilience of chieftaincy institutions (Fisiy 1995; Goheen 1992; Fisiy and Goheen 1998; Fokwang 2003, 2009; Williams 2004; Ubink 2007; Cheka 2008; Makahamadze, Grand & Tavuyanago 2009; Morapedi 2010; Dean 2013; Logan 2009, 2013; Cantell 2015), even in contexts like Mozambique where in the past they had been threatened with abolition (West & Kloeck-Jensen 1999; O'Laughlin 2000; Harrison 2002; Gonçalves 2002; Buur & Kyed 2005). A renewed boom in chieftaincy is thus observed and many chiefs are taking up central roles in contemporary politics (Harneit-Sievers 1998; Linchwe II 1989: 99-102; Bank & Southall 1996; van Rouveroy van Nieuwaal & van Dijk 1999; van Kessel & Oomen 1999; van Rouveroy van Nieuwaal 2000; van Binsbergen 2003a&b; Chabal, Feiman & Shalknik 2004; Angwafo III; Comaroff & Comaroff 2009:98-116; Fokwang 2009; Morapedi 2010; Logan 2009, 2013; Chakunda & Chikerema 2014; Owusu-Mensah 2014; Cantwell 2015).

In South Africa for instance, where even the ANC elite in struggle had predicted the passing of chieftaincy alongside apartheid (Mbeki 1984: 47; Maloka 1995, 1996; Hendricks & Ntsebeza 1999; Ntsebeza 2005) – notwithstanding the fact that chiefly cooperation with apartheid officials was not unanimous and unambiguous (Kelly 2015) – active dynamic re-appropriation of 'tradition' has been observed through claims to chieftaincy by historically marginalised cultural communities seeking recognition and representation (Oomen 2000a&b, 2003; Beall, Mkhize & Vawda 2005; LiPuma & Koelble 2009; Williams 2009; Mazibuko 2014; Kompi &Twala 2014), and chiefs like Mangosuthu Buthelezi have played and are playing key roles at the centre of post-apartheid party politics and power (Williams 2004, 2009; Beall 2005, 2006; Beall, Mkhize & Vawda 2005; Mazibuko 2014; Kompi &Twala 2014; Turner 2014). Although the empowerment of traditional authorities might make some anxious about a possible return to the bantustans of the apartheid era, where chiefs were divorced from their people and turned into high-handed dictators in the service of the dominant administration (Ntsebeza 2005; Oomen 2005)[1],

---

[1] See also Dr Mamphela Ramphele's critique of the Traditional Courts Bill (This is apartheid by another name, Sunday Times, 25 March

7

there is little reason to suggest that chiefs, like the rest of South Africans, are incapable of re-inventing themselves in post-apartheid South Africa. The resurgence of hereditary authority has resulted in or reactivated traditional tensions with bureaucratic authorities, especially at rural and local levels (King 2005; Beall 2005, 2006; Beall, Mkhize & Vawda 2005). As Jude Fokwang observed in an ethnographic study of the chiefdom of Tshivhase in the Limpopo Province, municipal councils presented as viable alternatives to chiefs assumed to be unaccountable because unelected, have turned out to offer little protection to the poor against the inequalities of the market, as they have bought wholesale into the post-apartheid rhetoric of the autonomous individual that is hardly in tune with the predicaments of the historically disadvantaged black poor. Confronted with the arbitrary, contradictory and often undemocratic tendencies of municipal authorities, 'Chief Tshivhase decided to back his subjects in refusing to pay for services they were not yet receiving', thereby proving himself to be more in tune with their predicaments than their 'elected' municipal councillors. Thus Fokwang's conclusion that such contradictions have created space for chiefs to fill, even if only on condition that they are able to draw from different kinds of legitimacy, and have not been discredited by past or present involvement with repressive states or agents (Fokwang 2003, Chapters 2, 3 &6)[2] The same is true of other countries in Africa, where even chiefs and chiefdoms discredited for past and present collaboration with repression, have, just like political parties

---

2012).

[2] The Limpopo Province alone has over 300 chiefs. Chief Kennedy Tshivhase, the most prominent of them, has occupied various portfolios in the ANC, including as senator in Cape Town and as provincial MP.

in liberal democratic contexts, refused to be permanently eclipsed in the game of legitimation. The acclamation or denunciation of African chiefs, like political choices everywhere, far from being a constant, is subject to renegotiation with the changing interests and fortunes of citizens, subjects and chiefs.

In general, chiefs and chiefdoms, instead of being pushed 'into the position of impoverished relics of a glorious past' (Warnier 1993: 318), have been functioning as auxiliaries or administrative extensions of many post-colonial governments, and as 'vote banks/brokers' for politicians keen on cashing in on the imagined or real status of chiefs as 'the true representatives of their "people" (Fisiy 1995: 49-50; Jua 1995; Mouiche 1992; Miaffo 1993; Oomen 2000a&b; Fokwang 2009; Logan 2009, 2013; Koter 2013). Although the presumed representability and accountability of chiefs to their populations have been questioned, this does not seem to have affected the political importance of chieftaincy in a significant way (Ribot 1999: 30-37). A growing number of scholars recognise chieftaincy as a force to be reckoned with in contemporary politics in Africa, especially with increasing claims for recognition, restitution and representation by cultural and ethnic communities. Whether or not a colonial creation, chieftaincy as a political and cultural identity marker is there to be studied, not dismissed. Many of us are yet to abandon our sterile prescriptiveness informed by the arrogance of ignorance, and to understand that the reductionist, insensitive, barbie-like model alternatives we seek to impose are simply too rigid to do justice to Africans and their communities as dynamic embodiments of a creative mix of encounters and identities. To be genuine scholars of democracy, we must be democratic in our scholarship, by emphasising observation over opinion.

The renewed scholarly interest in chieftaincy is a welcome development, since there is a need to counter the insensitivities or caricatures of certain abstract modernist discourses of mainstream theories and analysts that have tended, for ideological reasons, to rationalise chieftaincy and its dynamism away. It is important to develop approaches that are sensitive to the reality of intermediary communities between the individual and the state, and to the agency of chiefs and chiefdoms as individuals and cultural communities seeking 'rights and might' both as 'citizens' and 'subjects' in the coercive illusion that often passes for a 'modern nation-state'. Almost everywhere, chiefs and chiefdoms have become active agents in the quest by the 'modern big men and women' of politics, business, popular entertainment, bureaucracy and the intellect for traditional cultural symbols as a way of maximising opportunities at the centre of bureaucratic and state power (Geschiere 1993; Miaffo & Warnier 1993; Fisiy 1995; Goheen 1992; Fisiy & Goheen 1998; Eyoh 1998; Harneit-Sievers 1998; West & Kloeck-Jensen 1999: 460-475). It is in this connection that some scholars have understood the growing interest in the new elite to invest in neo-traditional titles and maintain strong links with their home village through kin and client patronage networks.

In Nigeria where chiefs remain active in politics despite a 1999 constitutional void on their position and role (Peter 2014), investment in chieftainship has become a steady source of symbolic capital for individuals who have made it in 'the world out there' (be it *4-1-9ly* or otherwise), and of development revenue by cultural communities who would otherwise count for little as players in their own right on national and global scenes (Harneit-Sievers 1998; Uwalaka 2014). In Ghana where the malleability and fluidity of chieftaincy accounts for its persistence, membership or association with chieftaincy enhances social status, facilitates contacts with politicians and foreigners, increases the possibility of going abroad and goes with a kind of political immunity (Knierzingern 2011). But almost everywhere, such participation and investment have led 'not to the reproduction, but rather to the transformation of the structures and relationships of power' (Goheen 1992: 406), and to creative negotiation and conviviality between continuities and encounters with change and innovation. Granted their persistence and influence in Africa, chieftaincy institutions need to be 'understood not only, and not even primarily, as belonging to a pre-modern, pre-capitalist past, but rather as institutions which have either (been) adapted to the contemporary socio-political setting, or even have been specifically created for or by it' (Harneit-Sievers 1998: 57). There is hardly any justification for labelling and dismissing chieftaincy *a priori* as unaccountable, when even the most touristic of observations would point to a fascinating inherent dynamic and negotiability that guarantees both resilience and renewal of its institutions (Comaroff 1978; van Binsbergen 2003a: 33-39; Comaroff and Comaroff 2009:98-116; Angwafo III 2009; Knierzinger 2011; Cook & Hardin 2013).

Such an ability to adapt and survive is not confined to chieftaincy in Africa. Monarchies the world over have demonstrated this resilience and adaptability of might in the face of clamours for rights. On June 5th 2002, watching from Gaborone in Botswana, I followed reports on the Golden Jubilee celebrations for Queen Elizabeth II on British

11

television (BBC and Sky News), hailing the fact that over one million people had braved the cold and rain to claim their space in history and the best in pageantry at Buckingham Palace in London. The Queen's love, glory and steadfastness were said to have earned her the respect of her subjects and the Commonwealth. The Queen's adaptiveness and stature as a symbol of unity were described by Prime Minister Tony Blair as the reason for the current outpouring of deference from people with whom she enjoys a strong and deep relationship. The British monarchy has survived also thanks to a shrewd investment of its symbolic capital in the new elite, some of whom have risen to prominence from among the working classes and inner-cities. By extending knighthood and lordship beyond the traditional realm of 'birthright' and 'blue blood' and to embrace achievements within the realms of modern politics, science, business, sports, the entertainment industry and other spheres of modern Britain, the monarchy has earned respect among its most likely critics. The institution has also sustained recognition in the Commonwealth through co-optation of Commonwealth elites into its orbit of symbolic power. The days of empire may be over, but the monarchy remains cherished by the British and the Commonwealth, thanks to its ability to deliver rights even as it continues to claim might.

This study argues that the rigidity and prescriptiveness of modernist partial theories have left a major gap in scholarship on chiefs and chieftaincy in Africa. It stresses that studies of domesticated agency in Africa are sorely needed if we are to capture the creative ongoing processes and to avoid overemphasising structures and essentialist perceptions on chieftaincy and the cultural communities that claim and are claimed by it. Scholarship that is impatient with the differences and diversities that empirical research highlights, runs the risk of pontification or orthodoxy. Such stunted or reductionist scholarship, like the rigid notions of liberal democracy mentioned earlier, is akin to the behaviour of a Lilliputian undertaker who would rather trim a corpse than expand his/her coffin to accommodate a man-mountain, or a carpenter whose only tool is a huge hammer and to whom every problem is a nail.

Too often we read scholarship of desire and expectations about Africa, rather than scholarship informed by what Africa actually is and by ongoing processes of negotiation of multiple identities by Africans. As many scholars have noted, there is hardly ever a discourse on Africa for Africa's sake, and others have often used Africa as a pretext for their own subjectivities, self-imagination and perversions (Comaroff, J. and J. 1997: 236-322; Magubane 2004; Schipper 1990: 12-13). No amount of new knowledge seems challenging enough to bury for good the ghost of simplistic assumptions about Africa. Only by creating space for scholarship based on Africa as a unit of analysis on its own right (Mamdani 1996: 8), could scholars begin to correct prevalent situations whereby much is known of what African states, institutions and communities '*are not*' (thanks to dogmatic and normative assumptions of mainstream scholarship) but very little of what '*they actually are*' (Mbembe 2001: 3-9). In other words, scholars on Africa ought to demonstrate less might and more right by being sensitive in theory and practice to the predicaments and realities of Africans as bearers and makers of history.

If we consider chiefs as agents and chieftaincy as dynamic institutions, we are likely to be more patient towards ongoing processes of negotiation, accommodation and conviviality between continuities and encounters with difference and innovation on the continent. We would be less keen on signing a death warrant for or seeking to bury chieftaincy alive. Africans have been quick to recognise the merits and limitations of liberal democracy and its rhetoric of rights, because they are inadequately accounted for under global consumer capitalism and because of the sheer resilience and creativity of their cultures. With this recognition has come the quest for creative ways of marrying tradition and modernity, ethnicity and statehood, subjection and citizenship, might and right. Such creativity has often resulted in largely misunderstood attempts at domesticating exogenously induced notions of democracy and accountability.

African communities are similar in numerous ways, just as they are diverse. I use the examples of Cameroon and Botswana to buttress my argument that Africans are far from giving up chieftaincy or from turning it into completely modern institutions. Like Africans elsewhere on the continent, Cameroonians and Batswana are simultaneously modernising their traditions and traditionalising their modernities. No one, it seems, is too 'citizen' to be 'subject' as well, not even in Southern Africa where modernisation *à l'occidentale* (westernisation if you like) is often claimed to have succeeded the most (Ferguson 1999: 1-81; Nyamnjoh 2001b). Invented, distorted, appropriated or not, chieftaincy remains part of the cultural and political landscapes, and is constantly negotiating and renegotiating with new encounters and changing material realities. The results are chiefs and chiefdoms that are neither completely traditional nor completely modern. Chiefs and chiefdoms shape and are shaped by the marriage of influences that makes it possible for Africans to be both 'citizens' and 'subjects', and to

14

negotiate conviviality among competing forces in their lives. Being African is neither exclusively a matter of tradition and culture, nor exclusively a matter of modernity and citizenship: it is being a melting pot of multiple encounters. This is what *Fon* Angwafo III of Mankon – my father, chief and informant means when he repeatedly tells me during conversations on tradition and modernity: 'As far as I can remember, our traditions have always been modern, our moderntities traditional' (Nyamnjoh 2002a; Angwafo III, 2009)[3].

---

[3] See also Waterman 1997, for a similar idea among the Yoruba.

Chapter 2

Chieftaincy and the Game of Legitimacy in Cameroon

There is little doubt that most of 'the present ambiguity and ambivalence towards local authorities' in Cameroon and Africa at large (Rowlands & Warnier 1988: 120) were created during colonialism (Mamdani 1996). In the Bamenda region for example, where powerful chiefdoms date back over 400 years, relations between chiefs and the German and British colonial authorities were marked by considerable ambivalence. Chiefs were often co-opted as individuals, disregarding the body of councillors that governed with them and had until then played a monitoring role. The customary policy-making process was thus often lost as chiefs took their lead more from the colonial administrative officers than from their indigenous 'political elite' (Lloyd 1965: 73). At the same time however, their mythical qualities as moral and sacred authorities gave chiefs room to manoeuvre vis-à-vis both the administration and their own people. They thus experienced all the problems associated with indirect rule: if they were perceived by the administration to be overtly in support of their people and institutions, they ran the risk of being sanctioned by the government; if, on the other hand, they cooperated too closely with the government, they ran the risk of alienating their people. They were often in a predicament, and learnt to play one interest group against the other as circumstances and personal interests dictated (Nkwi 1976: 135-170; cf. Nkwi & Warnier 1982; Nyamnjoh 1985; Rowlands and Warnier 1988: 120-1; de Vries 1998).

Elsewhere, the situation was much the same. France thus for instance created 'warrant chiefs' in acephalous societies in the southern half of French Cameroon (Gardinier 1963; Le Vine 1964), a region without a tradition of central government. In areas with chiefdoms, such as the North and the Bamileke region of the Eastern Grassfields, France tried to turn their chiefs into auxiliaries of the central administration. Where it met with resistance, France was quick to remove the chiefs in question and replace them with appointees of its own. Under this system, many chiefs 'lost their prerogatives' (Le Vine 1964: 91-98), including the Sultans of Bamun and Ngaoundere. The policy everywhere was the introduction of 'a French created system of local control' through 'a gradual erosion of the power of indigenous political authority' (Le Vine 1964: 91-98). Like Britain, France thus ran into problems of legitimacy with its appointed 'chiefs' and *conseils de notables* who, although imbued with authority and backed by the central administration, were not accepted by the people. This legal system 'encouraged differential treatment' of Cameroonians 'according to a cultural, rather than a legal yardstick' (Le Vine 1964: 91-104), thus laying the foundation for the distinction between 'citizens' and 'subjects' that has come to characterise the bifurcated state there like elsewhere in Africa (Mamdani 1996).

It is evident that the 'chieftaincy reforms' carried out by the French (Le Vine 1964: 97-98), were adopted with very little alteration by the one-party, post-colonial state (Nkwi 1976, 1979; Nyamnjoh 1985; Mouiche 1992, 1997; Fokwang 2003). Although at independence Ahidjo promised to 'draw the basic principles of African democracy' from 'our traditional chieftainship' (Ahidjo 1964: 31-3), the role chiefs were eventually made to play remained as peripheral, ambiguous and ambivalent as under France and Britain. The various chiefs were only seen as useful if they could serve as effective instruments for the implementation of government policies amongst their people.

In this light the government took a series of moves to ensure the attainment of its objectives. These included an invitation in 1966 for chiefs to rally round the unified party; the establishment of criteria for the award of a 'Certificate of Official Recognition by the Government' in 1967; a presidential warning in1969 to all chiefs who were seen to be reluctant to change; the abolition of the House of Chiefs in 1972; and a decree in 1977 defining the role of chiefs within the new 'nation-state' (Nkwi 1979: 111 115; Nyamnjoh 1985: 102 5). Thus while the pre-colonial autonomy of ethnic communities was not restored, chiefs were defined and treated largely as auxiliaries of the government, subservient to district and regional state administrative officers. This enabled central government to draw from chiefs as 'vote banks/brokers' often without having to credit them with effective power and active participation in decision making at local and national levels. Legally, the state 'guarantees the protection of chiefs and the defence of their rights while they are in office', but it also sanctions 'those chiefs who fail to live up to the laws of the nation-state.' Chiefs who fail to conduct their duties within the limits of the laws of the state 'can be made destitute or thrown out of their traditional office by government.' This dispensation remains largely unchanged, despite the political liberalisation and intensification in the politics of recognition that have since the 1990s increased competition for the attention of chiefs and chiefdoms by the political elite of different persuasions.

Some saw and continue to see in this 'a complete erosion' of the powers of chiefs who 'can only survive if they recognize and function according to the dictates of the new political elite' (Nkwi 1979: 115).

From these observations, it is clear that despite 'a disquieting variety of types of political organisation' in pre-colonial Cameroon (Rowlands & Warnier 1988: 120), little was done by the new ruling elite to question the colonial systems grafted onto the country by France and Britain. It was clearly in the interest of the new power elite (the intelligentsia included) to play down the importance of chieftaincy and 'tradition' as they sought to affirm their 'modern' authority. In the post-colony, the power of chiefs in regions where chieftaincy predated colonialism has continued to be 'undermined by the central authorities' while that of 'warrant chiefs' as colonial creations has been guaranteed largely by demonstrations of force against the local populations by the state, thus making the state out of touch with village communities (Rowlands & Warnier 1988: 120; Geschiere & Nyamnjoh 1998). Prior to the re-emergence of multipartyism in the 1990s, the ideology of nation-building and national unity meant that various ethnic groups saw their local and sectional loyalties and interests suppressed and were forced into a relationship of dependence on a highly centralised government (Bayart 1985). For the same reason, cultural communities or chiefdoms felt increasingly sidestepped and powerless: even with their most pressing problems and interests, such as the socio-economic changes which they were supposed to help realise, were planned and carried out or simply ignored, entirely without reference to them.

In the 1990s, however, the advent of multi-party politics forced the chiefs to make more open political commitments, thereby enhancing their potential for prominence at regional and national levels, even as their scope for manoeuvre appeared threatened. The chiefs were caught at the centre of the turbulent relations that characterised the modern power elite, part of which some chiefs had become as a result of their personal achievements in modern education. While it is commonplace to assume that chiefs were manipulated by the new power elite, it is worth researching the extent to which this assumption is true. Such claims deny the chiefs all agency in their actions, treat them as homogenous, and ignore the fact that political choices are predicated upon vested interests, which are not fixed, but subjected to re-negotiation with changing circumstances.

The overwhelming presence of central government and bureaucratic state power brought about great empowerment and opportunities for both individuals in general and dissenting individuals in particular. These opportunities have made the customary social structures of chiefdoms more ready to negotiate with, and accommodate, forms of agency and subjectivity that would certainly have been sanctioned into the margins in the past. On the other hand, successful individuals in the modern and individualistic sense, are just as ready to negotiate with and accommodate customary ideas of what I have referred to elsewhere as 'domesticated agency and intersubjectivity' - perhaps because of earlier socialisation into the collectivistic philosophy of their cultural group of origin, or because of awareness of the temporality and impermanence of personal success in the modern world, or perhaps because of both (Nyamnjoh 2002a). The consequent conviviality or interdependence is usually creatively negotiated, and serves as the basis of future customs, to be referred to and negotiated with by others in similar predicaments. Customs are thus not merely being modernised: modernity is being customised. The outcome of these processes is a triumph neither for 'tradition' nor for 'modernity' as distinct entities, but rather for the new creation to which a marriage of both has given rise: individuals and communities as repertoires, melting pots and negotiators of conviviality between multiple encounters or competing influences.

Thanks to such adaptability, policies of confinement and marginalisation by the state do not constitute a total and permanent eclipse. Chieftaincy has survived and continues to influence ongoing processes. Indeed, the idea that chiefs are marginalised and reduced to local level politics or mere auxiliaries of the administration must be put into perspective. This was much more the case during colonialism and the single-party years of the post-colony, than it is today under multipartyism and the politics of recognition. Especially since the 1990s, prominent chiefs have joined the elite ranks of the ruling party and government even at national level, some of them as members of the central committee, political bureau, government, and parliament, and others as chairmen of parastatals or governors of provinces. Some chiefs, admittedly pro-government, are so powerful that they act as if they were above the laws of the central state. The 'lamido' [chief] of Rey Bouba in Northern Cameroon is thus for instance known to own his own army and can arrest, beat and even kill, with impunity. Other chiefs sympathetic to the opposition have become part of the inner core of decision makers and strategists, both overtly and covertly. Increasingly, chiefs are part and parcel of the modern elite, and they are as much victims of manipulation as they are guilty of manipulating. If zombification is possible, mutual zombification is increasingly the reality.

Chieftaincy has thus had continued relevance. Evidence of this includes the following:

- An increasing number of highly educated young men, some with doctoral degrees from European and North American universities, are being enthroned chiefs of various communities throughout the country. Unlike during the 1950s and 1960s when educated chiefs were rare and *Fon* Angwafo III's 1953 Diploma in Agriculture was a conspicuous exception, few who have become chiefs since the 1980s are illiterate, and most were regular civil servants prior to, and even after, their enthronement. A good case in point of literacy and also of negotiability between the literate chief and his chiefdom is Fon Ganyonga III of Bali Nyonga. He returned from Germany with a Ph.D. in Social Anthropology (a rare achievement) and a German wife, and inherited and married many other wives in accordance with custom following his enthronement in 1985. Initially rejected by some custodians of custom, the German wife, a medical doctor, has earned recognition and endeared herself to the chiefdom by mastering the Bali Nyonga language and through contributions to community healthcare (Fokwang 2003: chapters 4 and 5).[1]

---

[1] In the neighbouring chiefdom of Batibo, Fon Mbah, another young educated chief, has stayed faithful to his only wife, despite pressure from his subjects to marry other wives, as is normal for a chief in the grassfields.

- Struggles over entitlement to vacant thrones are still rampant, and often require the intervention of the Ministry of Territorial Administration to resolve, even if in general it does so in favour of a pro-government candidate.

- Similarly, more and more modern elites do not seem satisfied with their achievements within the modern sector and bureaucratic state power, and are increasingly investing in neo-traditional titles of notability for symbolic capital. On becoming President in 1982, Paul Biya thus for instance succumbed to an offer by the chiefs of the Bamenda grassfields, to be crowned 'Fon of Fons' (Chief of Chiefs), a ritual with as much potential benefits for the President as it was for the chiefs and chiefdoms who crowned him.[2]

- The practice by Grassfield chiefs of appointing and installing representatives among their subjects in the diaspora is quite common (Goheen 1992; Geschiere and Nyamnjoh 1998; Tabapssi 1999). As 'sons and daughters of the soil' of various home villages, some urban elite do not hesitate to invite their village chiefs to preside over ceremonies and functions aimed at enhancing their chances in the cities where they live

---

[2] In 2000, the chiefs additionally collectively honoured Nico Halle, a prominent Douala-based lawyer from Awing in Bamenda, with the title of Ntumfo ('Chief's Messenger'), in recognition of distinguished contributions to the development of the North West Province. This honour must have sent the right message to President Biya who, in May 2004, appointed the lawyer as member of his national elections observatory. See also Orock 2014.

and work (Nyamnjoh 2002a). Various chiefs encourage cultural activities among urban migrants from their chiefdoms, and are often called upon to inaugurate cultural halls built by their subjects in cities.

- Ethnic elite associations proliferate in the corridors of power and resources seeking political and economic recognition and representation for their regions or peoples as cultural units (Nyamnjoh and Rowlands 1998; Nyamnjoh 1999). They do not hesitate to call upon their chiefs to facilitate this process of 'bringing development' to the home village (Konings 1996, 1999, 2003), even if this entails rivalry and conflict with other chiefdoms (Mouiche 1997; Mope Simo 1997; Fokwang 2003).

- Inter-ethnic conflicts over boundaries between chiefdoms have increased with the growth in the politics of belonging and 'primary patriotism' since the 1990s (Mope Simo 1997; Geschiere and Gugler 1998; Nyamnjoh and Rowlands 1998; Nyamnjoh 1999; Geschiere and Nyamnjoh 1998, 2000). Visiting the Buea and Yaounde archives for colonial maps and records on tribal territories and boundaries has become very popular, with urban elites assisting their chiefs with part-time research into histories.

The role chiefs played in the process of democratisation often determined their future position. In the Bamenda grassfields for example, this position was largely determined by anticipation and recognition of, or failure to attract, state-driven development efforts in their chiefdoms. With the pro-democracy clamours of the early 1990s, chiefs supporting the government felt this was the best way of securing state protection and safeguarding their interests in a context of keen competition and differences along ethnic lines. Put in a popular aphorism – 'politics na njangi' (Ngomba 2012; Nyamnjoh 2013): because the state had scratched, or promised to scratch, the backs of chiefs, it was only normal to return the compliment by scratching the back of the Head of State and ruling party. In the politics of give-and-take and a context of severe economic recession, it was out of the question not to hope to harvest where one had sown, and very dangerous to sow where one was not sure to harvest. Those chiefs who threw their weight behind the opposition parties, or claimed neutrality, tended to be quite critical of the government and ruling party for failure to bring development to their home areas, or for politicising chiefship through an arbitrary system of classification into first, second and third class chiefs. In supporting the opposition, disgruntled chiefs were hoping for a new political dispensation that would reinstate the dignity of chieftaincy and reward them accordingly. No position in reality was politically neutral, not even the one that proclaimed that chiefs should be above partisan politics.

Since the late 1990s, a diminishing number of chiefs have been openly in support of the opposition or the neutrality of chiefs in partisan politics. This tendency is in correspondence with the dwindling political fortunes of the Social Democratic Front (SDF)[3], the leading opposition party in the area and in

---

[3] In the early 1990s when the party was full of promise, its acronym 'SDF' was popularly translated to 'Suffer Don Finish' [our tribulations are over], but as the CPDM thwarted aspirations for transparent electoral

the country. With the intensification of the politics of belonging and ethno-regionalism since the amendment of the constitution to protect ethnic and regional minorities politically in 1996, Bamenda grassfields chiefs have mobilised themselves under various lobbies to demand more recognition and resources from government, often in opposition to the competing interests of their counterparts within the grassfields and in other regions. While the chiefs are generally conciliatory to the ruling party and government as 'the hand that feeds them and their chiefdoms' and would like to re-instate the House of Chiefs[4], there is fierce competition and rivalry among them for power and resources.

Pertaining to agency, certain chiefs, mostly those that are educated, have succeeded more than others in negotiating conviviality between modern and customary bases of power, and between the interests of the state and those of their chiefdoms. The talents, abilities, education, networks, connections and creativity of individual chiefs determine who succeeds with whom, where, how and with what effects.[5] Some have become part of the new elite at the centre of national and regional power. Through their individual capacities or via networks and various associations[6], these

---

democracy, the membership became disillusioned – 'Suffer Dey Front' [our tribulations are far from over], and the subject of jokes by CPDM militants – 'Small Die Fowl' [a dead little fowl].

[4] The House of Chiefs was abolished in 1972 in favour of the unitary state.

[5] *Fon* Doh Gah Gwanyin of Balikumbat was the only parliamentarian for the ruling Cameroon People's Democratic Movement (CPDM) of the opposition dominated North West province from 1997 – 2002.

[6] Such associations were the North West Fons' Union (NOWEFU) led by Fon Abumbi II John Ambe of Bafut, and the North West Fons' Conference (NOWEFCO) led by Fon Doh Gah Gwanyin of Balikumbat.

chiefs stake claims on national power and resources for their region and chiefdoms. *Fon* Angwafo III of Mankon for example, the most educated chief of his time, became the first chief to be elected MP in 1961 in a keenly contested multiparty election in which he ran as an independent (see Awasom 2003; Angwafo III, 2009). He ignored calls for his resignation as either MP or chief by those who thought it was improper for a chief (whose position is ascribed or by might) to hold an elected office (achieved or by right). From his defiance it was clear that he did not subscribe to the dichotomy between ascription and achievement, might and right, traditional and modern. Upon the re-unification of the English and French Cameroons in 1961, *Fon* Angwafo III became a member of the sole party, which he served as president of the Bamenda section. He stayed on as MP until his retirement from active politics in 1988. However, the launching of the SDF in Mankon and the dramatic resignation from the ruling CDPM in 1990 of John Ngu Foncha[7], brought *Fon* Angwafo III back to the centre of local and national politics. He was appointed to replace Foncha as the national vice-president of the CDPM. *Fon* Angwafo III has been described as 'a shining example of a pragmatist' (Aka 1984: 64), and a man of many faces who has skilfully married two different political cultures. He fails to see why chiefs should be treated as apolitical animals or placed above party politics, when they are citizens just like anyone else. He has repeatedly defended himself in interviews with the press and with researchers like myself (Nyamnjoh 2002a: 124-135),

---

[7] The Anglophone architect of re-unification and prominent statesman.

by asking: 'How can you deprive a citizen of involvement in politics simply because he holds a traditional title of *fon*?'.[8]

To maintain themselves as embodiments of particular cultural communities, chiefs constantly negotiate their positions within the contradictions between the state on the one hand, and in relation to competing expectations within the communities on the other (Konings 1996, 1999, 2003; Awasom 2003; Fokwang 2003, 2009; Warnier 1993, 2007; Cheka 2008). This is true not only of Cameroonian chiefdoms. Chiefdoms do not only continue to explore new ways of domesticating the agency and subjectivity of their 'sons and daughters' at the centre or periphery of modernity, but also adopt mechanisms to promote their communities for collective agency and intersubjectivity in changing situations. Such adaptability or dynamism is displayed both towards macro level changes, and towards developments within the family among youth and between genders. Continuity and change alike are determined by mutuality in concessions (Nyamnjoh 2002a; Angwafo III, 2009).

---

[8] For a Ghanaian parallel of chiefs in similar predicaments, especially in a context where the constitution formally bars chiefs from participating in 'active' politics, see Boafo-Arthur 2001; Valsecchi 2007; Knierzinger 2011; Anamzoya 2014.

Chapter 3

Chieftaincy and the Negotiation of Botswana's Democracy

Chieftaincy and chiefs in Botswana have displayed a similar agency to that noted among their counterparts in Cameroon, siding with forces that best guarantee their interests as communities and individuals, while hostile to those that radically threaten their might (Morton & Ramsay 1987: 11-60; Parsons et al. 1995; Selolwane 2002; Morapedi 2010; Cantwell 2015). Makgala traces this agency back to the colonial period when *Dikgosi* (chiefs) were able to reform the blanket model of the indirect-rule regime that had been introduced in 1935. They were enabled to do this through their insistence on the need to respect local political conditions (Makgala 1999: 11-97).

In 1948, Seretse Khama, the prince of the Bangwato chiefdom who had gone to study law at Oxford, married Ruth Williams, the daughter of an Anglican English family. The marriage was opposed by Khama's uncle Tshekedi[1], by Ruth's parents, by the apartheid regime in South Africa, and by the British colonial authorities. This resulted in Seretse Khama's banishment from Bechuanaland in 1950. Patient explaining and negotiation between might and right at various *dikgotla* [chiefs' council, assembly or parliament] eventually led to reconciliation, and the couple were finally accepted by

---

[1] As Bangwato regent, Tshedeki was firm: 'Drop your wife and be kgosi, or stay away with her and leave bogosi to me'. This firmness that made Seretse Khama suspicious: he believed that 'Tshekedi was trying to oust him to grab the chieftainship for himself' (Parsons et al. 1995: 78-79).

both Bangwato and the British government[2],who in 1955 allowed them to come home (Parsons et al. 1995: 75-149). Khama eventually served Botswana as its first president and he used his position as a lawyer, a devout liberal and as a chief to promote independence and nation-building. From independence in 1966, Khama's personal qualities guaranteed his ruling Botswana Democratic Party (BDP) regular electoral victories in both the Central District - his chiefdom - and throughout the country as a whole since. Commenting in a recent BTV documentary on Seretse Khama (Broadcast 9 June 2002), President Mogae described him as a principled person who insisted on people expressing their views, despite the fact that he could easily have been a dictator, given the amount of prestige and respect he enjoyed, and the fact that he was a chief. Khama's agency, which has been well documented (Parsons et al. 1995), and other examples provided below are yet further indications that scholars must avoid the tendency to mistake labels for substance, and to prescribe rather than observe.

The Khama factor in Botswana politics remains strong even after his death. In April 1998, when Festus Mogae took over as President from Sir Ketumile Masire[3] , Lt. General Ian Khama thus for instance retired as commander of the Botswana Defence Force to deploy his might as *kgosi* of Bangwato, in keeping the BDP of his late father together, and in maximising its fortunes at the 1999 general elections (Molomo 2000). The party's landslide victory was largely attributed to his appeal as *kgosi*, and his appointment as vice-

---

[2] For press recollections following the death of Lady Ruth Khama in May 2002, see *The Botswana Guardian*, 31 May 2002, 5 June 2002, The Botswana Gazette, 5 June 2002, and Mmegi Monitor, 4 June 2002.

[3] Note the 'Sir' in relation to the British Monarchy referred to above. Seretse Khama was also knighted by the Queen.

president after the election was regarded as a sign of gratitude by President Mogae. The decision to give Khama supervisory powers over other ministers so shortly after he returned from a controversial year-long sabbatical from politics, was explained in a similar manner. So also was his victory in the 2004 contest for the BDP chairmanship. Like his father, Khama has been able to negotiate and manipulate might and right in responding to competing claims on him as *kgosi*, MP, vice-president and party chairman by Batswana as 'citizens', 'subjects' or both. It is the same status of a popular *kgosi* that has blended productively with electoral democracy to make it possible for him to succeed president Mogae as head of state of Botswana.

Other *Dikgosi* have demonstrated similar agency and negotiability in their various chiefdoms and nationally (Morapedi 2010; Bauer 2014; Cantwell 2015). The popularity of the Botswana National Front (BNF) in the Bangwaketse chiefdom for example, is thus generally attributed to the traditional support the party has received from *Kgosi* Seepapitso Gaseitsewe, who in turn has attracted special attention and ambivalence from the BDP government, which has been keen on improving its image in the chiefdom. *Kgosi* Seepapitso Gaseitsewe's appointment as Botswana's ambassador to the UN in 2001 was seen by some as an attempt by government to keep the outspoken and critical chief out of the way.

Despite their relative economic success and advances in modernisation, most Batswana continue - in the face of the contradictions of liberal democracy - to be attracted to customary ideas of leadership, and they realise that pursuing an undomesticated autonomy is a rather risky business. There is an ever-looming possibility, even for the most successful

33

and cosmopolitan of Batswana, of sudden unexplained failure and of having to cope alone. This explains people's eagerness to maintain kin networks they can fall back on in times of need and misfortunes, insurance schemes notwithstanding (Ngwenya 2000).

The long arm of custom and chieftaincy has refused to leave migrants alone, just as migration has failed to provoke a permanent severing of relations with the home village and its institutions. Civil servants, politicians, chiefs, intellectuals, and academics are all part of this quest for cultural recognition even as they clamour for the entrenchment of their rights as citizens in a Botswana state. Continued interest in chieftaincy by various elites and elite associations is a good indication of such commitment to community and cultural identities beyond the voluntary associations of the liberal democratic type. Elites from majority and minority ethnic groups alike have created associations such as the Society for the Promotion of Ikalanga Language, Pitso Ya Batswana, and Kamanakao to articulate their claims to chiefs, paramountcy and cultural representation, even as the logic of modernisation theorists would portray them uniquely as 'citizens' of 'a liberal democracy' (Werbner 2002a, b & c; Werbner and Gaitskell 2002).

The following examples further illustrate the dynamics of chieftaincy in Botswana, regardless of the requiems that prescriptive and normative scholarship has sung in this regard.

Case One: Dikgosi and Marriage
In Tswana chiefdoms, the politics, management, flexibility and negotiability of marriage are well documented (Schapera [1938] 1994: 125-184; cf. Comaroff 1981).

34

Chieftaincy contains conservative and progressive forces within its ranks on various issues, and its survival depends a lot more on negotiation and conviviality between the forces than on revolutions or insensitivities to the interests of others. There is a generational dimension to how various chiefs perceive the importance of marriage. The older chiefs see marriage as duty to the chiefdom, while the younger generation see marriage as a personal matter to be realised by the individual chief only when he has found the right woman to make him happy as a husband. Yet despite the public display of difference between the older and youthful chiefs, the very fact that the institution tolerates and provides for both married and unmarried chiefs is evidence of how conciliatory towards custom and innovation chieftaincy is. It guarantees survival for itself by posing as a melting point for competing perspectives on marriage and its role in present-day Botswana.

It is Saturday 23 February 2002, at Goodhope. The occasion is the enthronement of 25 year-old Lotlamoreng II Montshioa, as *Kgosi* of Barolong. With his enthronement Lotlamoreng will become one of the youngest paramount chiefs in Botswana. The issue of the day is Lotlamoreng's unmarried status. *Kgosi* Linchwe II of Bakgatla (Cantwell 2015)[4], oldest paramount chief, revered custodian of culture, and president of the Customary Court of Appeal in Botswana, expresses concern over the rapid transformations and the loss of dignity in chieftaincy. He claims that the onus of restoring the dignity of chieftainship lies with the chiefs themselves, especially with the young breed of chiefs who have lost respect by staying unmarried. He says that in their

---

[4] For some of his achievements in relation to the South African liberation struggle, 1948-1994.

days, a young *Kgosi*-to-be had to be married, 'so that your tribe can respect you.' Turning to *Kgosi* Tawana II, another young, unmarried chief who is also Chairman of the House of Chiefs, Linchwe says: 'You have to marry. We must know where *Dikgosi* wake up each morning, not to be emerging from shacks all over the village. You must be flanked by your wife on occasions like this one. [....] This way, you have dignity with your people and they respect you.' He adds: 'I am touched, *Kgosi ga e a tshwanela mo morafeng* [A Chief should not be coming in the company of a girlfriend in a public place].'

Kgosi Linchwe's reputation is such that few dare contradict him. But *Kgosi* Tawana is used to talking back. Turning to Lotlamoreng, he says: 'Take your time before getting married, so that when you marry you do so for your own benefit and the benefit of your family, not for Barolong and other people.' He stresses that *Dikgosi* must separate their private lives from their duties, and drawing from his own experience, he adds: 'Life is yours and live it the way you feel comfortable. Don't allow yourself to be under pressure from anybody. You live for yourself, your mother and your family and not your tribe. I made that mistake six years ago when I became chief. I thought my life was inseparable from the Batawana, but suddenly I realised that I had my own life to live. When it is time for you to settle, then you will have chosen the woman who will make you a happy husband - and not one you would leave for other women and schoolgirls. Six years ago, I would not have liked to bring a woman into the Moremi poverty, that is why I am ready to do so now.'

Also critical of unmarried *Dikgosi* is the Minister of Local Government, Dr Margaret Nasha: 'I am pleading with you to go out there and find a wife to wed. I will be waiting anxiously to get news that you are getting married; that is when I will bring you a present, not today.' *Kgosi* Lotlamoreng replies: 'I have been listening to Minister Nasha and *Kgosi* Linchwe attentively, but while I respect them I agree with my chairman, *Kgosi* Tawana. As you all know I have been Chief for a short time only and I think it won't be wise for me to wed before some of the elders'.

Commenting after the ceremony, *Kgosi* Linchwe says that he was taken by surprise by the remarks made by *Kgosi* Tawana, claiming that these were not in order. 'A chief should lead by example, if he marries, the tribe will follow suit and the nation will be kept.' Linchwe says that *Kgosi* Tawana 'should know that when a chief is given royal counselling, it is abominable for him or anybody to answer back. If you answer back or engage in the game of theorising on the merits and demerits of the advice given, you run the risk of defeating the advice and the sacred exercise. I do not think many would share Tawana's sentiments because it is a given in our culture that adults, let alone chiefs should marry.'

Tawana continues to be equally adamant after the ceremony, claiming his conscience is clear. 'A *Kgosi* should not just marry because he is *Kgosi*, he should marry only when he is ready and not because there is pressure.' He denies he has problems with *Kgosi* Linchwe, claiming instead that '*Kgosi* Linchwe has always been a father figure to me and he will remain so. He is a very close family friend.'[5] The difference of perception between them on the issue of marriage could perhaps be the result of 'a generation gap', he speculates.[6]

---

[5] Linchwe knew Tawana's father well: they were friends during their school days in England. Linchwe considers Tawana his son and he is always ready to give him advice.

[6] The Midweek Sun, 27 February 2002, 'Lotlaamoreng Claims his Right', by Abdul Salaam Moroke, p. 3, The Botswana Gazette, 27 February 2002, 'To Marry or not: Lotlaamoreng gets varied advice', by

Shortly after the incident *Kgosi* Tawana reportedly announced his intention to marry Tsitsi Orapeleng of Palapye, his girlfriend since 1998, with whom he has a two-year old son, in January 2003 (Mmegi, 29 March 2002, by Lekopanye Mooketsi, p. 7). Around the same period, the press reported that preparations were underway for Lt General Ian Khama to marry his South African girlfriend, Nomsa Mbere, a practising dentist in Gaborone.[7]

Case Two: The First Female Paramount Kgosi

One of the arguments advanced against chieftaincy in Africa is the assertion that it is a predominantly male institution. The prevalence of male chiefs has been used as proof of the undemocratic nature of the institution, often in total disregard of subtle and overt mechanisms against autocratic tendencies on the part of chiefs and males. If one were to take this caricature for reality, the following case would seem to suggest that even this pillar (male-centredness) of chieftaincy is not beyond renegotiation. In other words, the fact that chieftaincy has been dominated by men in the past does not imply that it cannot be reformed to accommodate women. Here again, we see an institution that is adaptable and negotiating with changing political and social realities in Botswana. A woman claiming her 'birthright' as a 'citizen' as provided for in Botswana's constitution and stressing her leadership skills within the 'modern' service

---

Tshepo Molwane, p. 3, Mmegi Monitor, 26 February 26 2002, 'Tawana and Linchwe in a Tiff', by Enole Ditsheko p. 9, Mmgei, 1 March 2002, 'Do not come in public with a girlfriend', 'Linchwe, live life the way you feel', by Gideon Nkala p. 10.

[7] See Mmegi Monitor, 2 April 2002, 'Khama Confirms His Marriage', by Letshwiti Tutwane pp. 2, 9 Aprl 2002, 'Bangwato ask for Khama's wife', by Kagiso Sekokonyane p. 2.

industry, is able to access a position customarily defined by 'might' and predominantly traced through the male descent line. The outcome, once again, is neither victory for 'tradition' nor 'modernity', but for Batswana as individuals and groups for whom 'right and might' taken together offer the best protection against the dangers of unmitigated dependence on either.

Mosadi Muriel Seboko was born in Ratmostwa in 1950 as first child to the late Paramount *Kgosi* Mokgosi III. She was educated at Moedin College, where she completed her Cambridge Overseas School Certificate in 1969. She joined Barclays Bank in 1971, where she later became department manager and administrator. In 1995, she retired from Barclays, after 24 years of service. In 2001 she worked as floor manager with Century Office Supplies in Broadhurst. Mosadi is mother of four children who are currently pursuing their own careers.

In an interview with Gary Wills of *The Botswana Gazette* newspaper in November 2001, Mosadi Seboko explained, *inter alia*, why she wanted to be the paramount *kgosi* of Balete. 'The main reason is that as the eldest child in the family of [...] *Kgosi* Mokgosi III this is my birthright. Thus, it's only fair that I inherit what I strongly believe belongs to me. Secondly, I also do not doubt my capacity to lead my tribe and I believe I'm fit in all respects for such a demanding post. I have no criminal record and certainly there are no skeletons in my cupboard!'

Asked why she, a woman, wanted to become chief in a country where this was considered the prerogative or birthright of men, she replied: 'Because of the rather patriarchal system practised in Botswana, culturally, people believe a woman cannot lead her tribe as a paramount chief.

However, the Constitution of Botswana does not discriminate against women due to their sex. My understanding of the Bill of Rights in the Constitution suggests that actually we have equal rights as men and women, to such positions.'

And to prove that she would make an excellent chief, she was bringing some important skills and experience to the position, she said:

> In my previous jobs I've had the opportunity to handle, manage and supervise people. This has given me capacity to discharge and develop my human resource management skills. Since the chieftainship is highly people-oriented this experience is important, and having been involved with a service industry this has helped me work with people and consider their needs. And … I've also brought up children, including of course, helping my mother with my younger sisters and brother (the Late *Kgosi* Seboko) that is, after my father *Kgosi* Mokgosi III, died rather prematurely.

Before her eventual appointment, Mosadi Seboko felt that her appointment would have a positive impact on women in Botswana and beyond. 'As regards the impact on other women I do feel this will be a plus, especially concerning the empowerment of women. … [W]omen's NGO's have, for a long time, lobbied government to look at all sectors with respect to gender neutrality, and this must include the chieftainship.' Among her supporters has been the women's movement represented by organisations such as Emang Basadi. She has also received encouragement and great support 'from the public in the village, especially the headmen in different wards,' and 'from individuals around the country, many of whom are in positions of responsibility.'

Her popularity notwithstanding, Mosadi Seboko blamed delays in her appointment on:

(…) the fact that the acting chief, and his team, appear not to accept my wish to become the next paramount chief of the Balete. Actually, they have not taken this issue very well and are not affording it the neutrality that it needs. Obviously, their campaign has been brought to my notice, both from various newspaper articles and through comments I hear from other people. For example, the acting chief Tumelo Seboko stated recently that he would be putting forward Tsimane Mokgosi's name (who is my young cousin) as the 'chief designate'. I assume that this is simply because he is male? What other reason could there be? However, he has promised to inform the tribe that I have expressed a desire to become the chief, and a meeting is planned this coming Saturday [1st of December 2001] at the main *kgotla* in Ramotswa.[8]

On 7 January 2002, *Kgosi* Mosadi Seboko officially took up duty as paramount *kgosi* of Balete, following approval of her appointment by the Minister of Local Government, Dr Margaret Nasha. The minister praised Balete 'for being progressive and breaking with tradition by allowing a woman to take the reigns of traditional power', and called upon other [tribes] to emulate the example. At a well-attended *kogtla*

---

[8] See Wills, G., The Botswana Gazette, 28 November 2001, pp. 16, 'With Mosadi Seboko: (A Gazette Exclusive) – Gary Wills Talks to A Serious Contender for the Balete Chieftainship'.

meeting in Ratmotswa in December 2001, during which Mosadi was elected to succeed her brother, *Kgosi* Seboko, who died earlier the same year, the minister confirmed the choice made by the people of Balete. Nasha's approval made of Mosadi Seboko the first woman substantive paramount *kgosi* in the history of Botswana.[9]

Reacting to discontent among 'tribal male chauvinists', *Kgosi* Mosadi said: 'What Balete need is a leader. Whether the leader is a man or a woman is immaterial. The key thing is education. People need to be educated to understand that a woman is capable of being a *kgosi*. Other than the unwritten customary rites and practices, *bogosi* [chieftainship], is mainly administrative. As a former administrator, I do not anticipate problems in my new profession as *kgosi*'.[10] Kgosi Seboko believes that her appointment corrects an anomaly that has been allowed to fester for years as women were relegated to positions inferior to those of men under the guise that the woman's position is behind the man. 'When I assumed office, I never thought for once that I would need to prove to Balete that I am as capable as my brothers were. I know that as a human being I am not infallible. All I am asking of my people and Batswana is to realise that and not to crucify me when I err only because I am a woman.'

On 28 January 2002, *Kgosi* Mosadi Seboko and *Kgosi* Letlamoreng II were both sworn into the House of Chiefs in accordance with legislation, which expects members of the house to be recommended first by their ethnic community and endorsed by the minister of local government. Some

---

[9] See the Botswana Gazette, 9 January 2002, p. 4, 'Mosadi Seboko is officially paramount chief of the Balete'.

[10] See Mmegi, 11 January 2002, "Tribal male chauvinists don't worry me" - Mosadi', pp. 8-9.

press reports claimed that '(…) Balete's new paramount chief *Kgosi* Mosadi Seboko rewrote the history of the House of Chiefs (…) [as] the first female paramount chief to take an oath of allegiance as a member of the house' (Midweek Sun 2002: 5).

In a 2014 study Gretchen Bauer (Bauer 2014; see also Matemba 2005) provides a rich and detailed account not only of how *Kgosi* Mosadi Seboko has fared since becoming the first woman paramount chief in Botswana, but also evidences the extent to which she and others have used their positions and power to foster the interest of women in the House of Chiefs and other avenues.

Case Three: Succession Disputes

Although succession disputes and competition for power 'have occurred with remarkable frequency' in Tswana and other Southern African chiefdoms, scholars have tended not to endorse this 'as sufficiently important to warrant a re-assessment of underlying assumptions' about chieftaincy as all might and no right (Comaroff 1978: 1). In his study of Barolong boo Ratshidi of South Africa, a sister chiefdom to Barolong of Botswana, John Comaroff observed that not only was 'competition for power (…) a ubiquitous feature of everyday politics, (…) neither precluded by rule nor limited to interregna', rules could not 'be assumed to determine the outcome of indigenous political processes'. Indeed, was succession to be exactly according to prescription, Comaroff estimated that 80 per cent of all cases of accession to the Barolong boo Ratshidi chiefship would have represented anomalies. He also noted that 'while access to authority is determined by birth, political power depends upon individual ability', and that a significant amount of power in practice is

43

wielded by recruited 'talented office-holders'. Thus, 'although entitled to formal respect and ceremonial precedence', the chief 'is regarded as a fallible human being who may or may not be powerful, and who may rule efficiently or ineptly'. Placing 'a high value upon consultation and participatory politics' as the chiefdom does, would ensure that even an incompetent chief benefits from 'the advice of his subjects, whether it be proffered informally or in public' (Comaroff 1978: 1). Just as power by vote does not preclude resort to might, power by birth does not obviate participation by right.

Similar negotiation and manipulation of legitimacy have been frequent among the Tswana of Botswana. Present-day Botswana is characterised by numerous disputes over succession among majority and minority 'tribes' alike. This points not only to chieftaincy as an institution that marries might and right in fascinating ways, but also highlights its continued importance in Botswana. Of the eight Tswana chiefdoms with permanent representation in the House of Chiefs, most have experienced disputes over succession to the throne. The Bakwena have thus for instance been plagued by such disputes, recently epitomised by a bitter legal wrangle between Kgari Sechele and his cousin Kealeboga Sechele, over who should be *Kgosi* of Bakwena. As the story goes, Kealeboga's grandfather, *Kgosi* Sebele II was deposed by British colonialists and replaced with his younger brother *Kgosi* Sechele III who was more agreeable to them. Sebele was banished from Bakwena territory and he died in exile (Morton and Ramsay 1987: 30-44). In 1962 Sebele's son, Moruakgomo made an effort to regain the throne to his family but failed. Upon his death, *Kgosi* Sechele III was succeeded by Bonewamang Sechele whose four-year old son, Kgari Sechele was designated heir apparent following his own death in 1978. Kgosikwena Sebele, uncle to Kgari Sechele, was appointed regent while waiting for Kgari to come of age, and served in that capacity for 16 years. The descendants of deposed *Kgosi* Sebele II have never given up their struggle to regain the throne. After Moruakgomo's abortive attempt in 1962, his younger brother Mokgaladi instituted fresh legal proceedings to reclaim the throne in 1999. When the latter died in 2000, his son Kealeboga Sechele continued with the claim, describing Kgari Sechele's designation as 'irregular and accordingly null and void', and thus arguing that he is the rightful heir following the death of his father Mokgalagadi.[11]

In March 2002 however, Kgari Sechele III was sworn in at the House of Chiefs, taking over from Kgosikwena Sebele, who had served as regent for 16 years, and who resigned in January 2002. Kealeboga tried in vain through his lawyer to stop the swearing in,[12] and Kgosikwena was not happy with initiatives taken by Kgari supporters without consulting him. In 2000 he was instructed by the Ministry of Local Government to make arrangements for Kgari Sechele's assession to the throne. He disobeyed the instructions on the grounds that another Bakwena royal, Mokgalagadi, was also a claimant to the throne on behalf of his son, Kealeboga. Instead, he called upon the Minister of Local Government to appoint a judicial commission of enquiry, as provided for in the law. The Minister refused, insisting that Kgosikwena must make way for Kgari's enthronement. Kgosikwena took the matter to court, which ruled against him, seeing no credible doubt to Kgari's legitimacy as heir to the throne. The court

---

[11] See The Midweek Sun, July 3, 2002, p. 4, 'Bakwena chieftainship case takes off', by Marcos Matebele.

[12] See Mmegi, March 29, 2002, p. 7; The Botswana Guardian, December 21, 2001; The Botswana Gazette, January 30, 2002, p. 6.

did not understand 'why the applicant was so stubborn as to consult the very tribe upon which his power must largely depend.' The court also wondered why Kgosikwena, in full knowledge, had delayed for 21 years before raising his doubts about Kgari's legitimacy as heir apparent. Kgosikwena resigned as regent following the court decision, which he appealed (The Botswana Guardian 2002: 6).

Commenting on a delegation of Bakwena elders to Serowe (home of Kgari's mother) to update the Bangwato royal family on preparations for Kgari's enthronement, Kgosikwena said: 'I don't know who sent them to Serowe because I am the one who is the contact between the tribe and the royal family. All communication between these two parties has to go through me. I also hear that last month Kgari was formally introduced to the tribe in the *kgotla*. How can that be when I am the one who is supposed to do that?' He was also opposed to the enthronement of Kgari before the court had decided on the dispute over succession. 'The case of who is the rightful heir to the throne is still before the High Court and at this stage it is premature to be talking about - let alone making preparations, for anyone's installation. When the High Court rules, either in Kgari or in Kealeboga's favour, it is only then that we can start talking about installing the next Bakwena paramount chief and sending delegations to other tribes.' (The Midweeek Sun 2002: 4) This claim is made despite the Chieftaincy Act, Section 25 of which states that no court shall have jurisdiction to hear and determine any matter concerning chieftainship, particularly with regard to the designation, recognition, appointment or suspension of chiefs. Amid this controversy, Kgari's enthronement was scheduled for and finally took place on August 17, 2002 (The Midweek Sun

2002: 5). While 'kingmaking' is clearly open to subjectivity and manipulation by 'king makers', being legitimate is not entirely about being more deserving, especially as less deserving and arbitrarily designated chiefs can over time earn legitimacy in their own right (Moseki 2003).

Case Four: Minority Tribes Fighting for Dikgosi and Representation

The claim that chieftaincy is generally unpopular and outmoded, is hardly reflected by the growing clamours by minority tribes for recognition and representation through chiefs of their own. Chiefdom status remains the ultimate symbol of identity and freedom in the plural context of modern Botswana, making a 'difference' and 'belonging to given cultural communities' a more convincing indicator of citizenship than the illusion of a unifying national culture that in effect thrives on inequalities and thinly disguises hierarchies among the Batswana. Of late, ethnic minorities in Botswana have been struggling to shake off the 'unifying' Tswana culture, and strive for individual recognition and representation.

What is important in the case of minority tribes articulated below is the fact that these groups see paramount chieftaincy as a solution to their marginalisation as cultural communities in Botswana. Through this they believe they could have the cultural recognition and representation they seek as citizens of modern Botswana with a given cultural heritage. In other words, while they appreciate their political rights as individual citizens in modern Botswana, they lament their collective subjection to Tswana culture. Hence the clamour for paramount chiefs of their own, and the refusal to endorse the argument that chieftaincy is an outmoded institution in a modern context of rights. For just how can chieftaincy be outmoded when thanks to chieftaincy some tribes are better recognised and represented than others?

The concern of the minority groups is more than just a rumour. Since the late 1980s, they have actively been seeking equal recognition as 'ethnic' or 'tribal' entities with paramount chiefs of their own, and with a right to representation in the House of Chiefs on equal terms with the Tswana *Dikgosi*. Newspapers abound with stories of various ethnic minority groups, hitherto represented by headmen and subchiefs, asking for their own paramount chief as a 'tribe' in their own right. As recently as June 15 2002, the remains of Bakalanga *She* (Chief) John Madawu Mswazwi, who died in exile in Zimbabwe in 1960, were reburied with pomp and ceremony in the Central District, in the presence of Botswana Television and Vice-President Ian Khama, whose granduncle Tshekedi Khama, as regent of the Bangwato chiefdom under which the Bakalanga are a minority ethnic group, had instigated his banishment by the colonial government. While Khama called for reconciliation in the interest of national unity, Bakalanga elite celebrated a milestone in their struggles for recognition and representation, even if this was short of the apology they wanted from Khama 'for the wrongful banishment of their chief'.[13] Bakalanga are one of the leading minority groups claiming cultural recognition and representation in Botswana (cf. Werbner 2002a, b & c).

Ethnic minorities have thus taken up the issue of the Botswana constitution, which appears to favour some groups to the detriment of others (Mazonde 2002; Durham 2002; Solway 2002; Werbner 2002a,b&c; Nyati-Ramahobo 2002). Of recent, the provisions of sections 77, 78 and 79 of

---

[13] See editorial in Mmegi Monitor, June 25, 2002, p. 10.

Botswana's constitution have formed the focus of the minority struggles, as the minorities claim that these sections only mention the eight Setswana speaking 'tribes', thereby relegating all other tribes to a minority status, and providing a basis for discrimination along ethnic lines. Evidence of such discrimination includes:

- inequalities of access to tribal land and administration;

- an educational and administrative policy that privileges the use of Setswana to the detriment of 20 minority languages, thereby denying the latter the opportunity to develop and enrich Botswana culturally; and

- unequal representation of cultural interests in the House of Chiefs, which is responsible for advising government on matters of tradition, custom and culture.

Critics of the constitution on these aspects have argued that such discrimination is contrary to the spirit of democracy and equality of citizenship (Selolwane 2000: 13, Mazonde 2002).

One of the minority groups that have been at the forefront of this struggle is the Bayei (also known as Wayeyi). The Bayei have been resisting their subjugation by Batawana for a long time, and they have sought recognition for a paramount chief of their own (Murray 1990; Nyati-Ramahobo 2002; Durham 2002). In the words of their leader

Shikati Calvin Kamanakao I:[14] 'We all deserve to be recognised as different tribal groupings who together make a whole called Botswana. We cannot achieve unity by denying other groups their identity, the age of serfdom and domination has long passed' (Mmegi Monitor 2002: 4).

In November 2001, the Bayei Kamanakao elite association won a partial victory when the High Court ruled in favour of its challenge that Section 2 of the Chieftaincy Act, which mentions only 'eight tribes', discriminated against minority ethnic groups like Bayei and needed amendment 'to afford equal treatment and equal protection by the law' to all chiefdoms or tribes.[15] In the words of the presiding Chief Justice, the Chieftaincy Act had '(…) serious consequences, when it is remembered that this Act is one of the laws that define which tribal community can be regarded as a tribe, with the result that such a community can have a chief who can get to the House of Chiefs and that only a tribe can have

---

[14] It is noteworthy that Calvin Kamanakao's leadership has not been uncontested. Kamanakao's legitimacy as Shikati [chief] of Bayei has been challenged by Moeti Moeti, through his father Jacob Moeti who is headman of the main Bayei ward in Maun. In a letter summoning Jacob Moeti to a Kgotla meeting to explain his claim, Lydia Nyati-Ramahobo, coordinator of the Kamanakao Association, wrote: 'We value our chieftaincy, for which we have struggled since time immemorial', and 'are not happy to have it dragged in the mud with such a sense of irresponsibility. We therefore wish to afford both of you an opportunity to tell the Wayeyi people in an open, transparent and democratic fashion, the origins of his [Moeti junior's] claims.' She warned that 'failure to attend will not prohibit the proceedings of the meeting and the conclusions reached would be final', and needed to 'help Wayeyi to achieve their freedom' (Mmegi Monitor 2002: 4).

[15] See The Botswana Gazette, November 28, 2001, pp.5, 'Partial victory for Bayeyi: Chief Justice agrees that Chieftainship Act discriminates against them, but declines to scrap constitutional provisions'.

land referred to as tribal territory.'[16] Following the ruling, Dr Lydia Nyati-Ramahobo, chairperson of the Kamanako Association, reportedly remarked: 'We are now equal to the Batawana; we are no longer a minority group.'[17]

The ruling in this case should be regarded within the framework of on-going debates on discriminatory sections of the constitution, which the Kamanakao had also challenged, but on which the court declined to rule. Previously, in July 2000, President Festus Mogae had appointed the Balopi Commission to investigate discriminatory articles of the constitution and in March 2001, the commission reported its findings (Republic of Botswana 2000: 93-110). A subsequent draft white paper, based on the commission's, findings argued that '(…) it makes sense to remove the *ex-officio* status in the membership of the House and subject each member of the House to a process of designation by *morafe* [tribe]. The same individual may be re-designated for another term if *morafe* so wishes.' It additionally stated that '(…) territoriality rather than actual or perceived membership of a tribal or ethnic group should form the fundamental basis for representation in the House of Chiefs.'

The draft white paper thus suggested that the discriminatory sections of the constitution were to be replaced with new sections 'cast in terms calculated to ensure that no 'reasonable' interpretation can be made that they discriminate against any citizen or tribe in Botswana'. It

---

[16] It should also be seen in line with the decision by the Ministry of Local Government to amend the Chieftaincy Act in accordance with the High Court judgement.

[17] See the Botswana Gazette, 28 November 2001, pp. 5, 'Partial victory for Bayeyi: Chief Justice agrees that Chieftainship Act discriminates against them, but declines to scrap constitutional provisions', The Midweek Sun, 28 November 2001, p. 3.

additionally endorsed the creation of new regional constituencies, 'which are neutral and bear no tribal or ethnic sounding names'. Regions were to have electoral colleges of Headmen of Record up to Head of Tribal Administration to designated members, and each region was to be entitled to one member of the House. The President would appoint three special members 'for the purpose of injecting special skills and obtaining a balance in representation.'

The finding of the Balopi Commission's and the suggestions in the draft white paper were much more readily accepted by the minority groups than by the majority Tswana, with vested interests in the status quo. The Tswana argued that the recommended alterations were aimed at eroding chieftaincy by emphasising territoriality over birthright, and at dividing the nation by 'placating minority tribes to the detriment of the rights of tribes that are mentioned in the Botswana Constitution'.[18] Particularly distasteful to the major tribes was the amendment of certain sections of the constitution, and membership of the House of Chiefs.

As a reaction to this criticism, President Mogae, himself an affiliate of a minority tribe and thus a supporter of the suggested alterations (The Batalaote), embarked on a nationwide tour of different *kgotla* to explain the issue. It was reported however, that, under pressure from the major tribes, Mogae backtracked on some key aspects of the draft white paper. In a 'war-of-words' meeting with the majority 'tribe' the Bangwato, the President was for instance told that 'It is of course fair that some [minor] tribes should be represented at the House of Chiefs, but their chiefs should still take orders from Sediegeng Kgamane [acting paramount chief of

---

[18] See the Botswana Gazette, April 10, 2002, p. 5 and April 3, 2002, p. 2; see also Mmegi Monitor, March 26, 2002, p. 2.

Bangwato]. We do not want chiefs who will disobey the paramount chief and even oppose him while there [in the House of Chiefs].'[19]

Mogae subsequently appointed a panel to redraft some of the white paper's more relevant sections, such as more equal representation in the House of Chiefs and the changing of the names of some regions, in time for submission to parliament. The revised white paper, which was eventually adopted by parliament in May 2002, re-introduced *ex-officio* chiefs as 'permanent' members, and it raised the number of House of Chief members from the current eight to twelve, which increased the total membership of the House of Chiefs to 35 members. It was foreseen that the four additional *ex-officio* members would be chiefs from the districts of Chobe, Gantsi, North East and Kgalagadi. These chiefs would be elevated to paramount status, while the traditional position of the eight from the Tswana tribes would be maintained (The Botswana Guardian 2002: 8.).

The revised white paper was rejected by most minority tribes, some of whose elite petitioned President Mogae, claiming that the changes were 'cosmetic', and accusing the government of having succumbed to pressure from Tswana tribes to ignore the findings of the Balopi Commission. The authors of the petition argued that 'As a general issue, we are rather not happy with the fact that while the Tswana-speaking tribes were consulted and indeed some modification made on the basis of their inputs before the paper was adopted by Parliament, the non-Tswana were consulted after the paper was adopted. This served as a psychological oppression to

---

[19] See the Midweek Sun, May 1, 2002, p. 3; Mmegi Monitor, April 2, 2002, p. 2.

disillusion these tribes. It reflected on the ethnic imbalance, as to who gets listened to in this country and who does not.'

They argued that the revised and adopted white paper had merely entrenched Tswana domination over other tribes, by simply translating from English into Setswana words such as 'House of Chiefs' (*Ntlo Ya* Dikgosi) and 'Chief' (*Kgosi*), oblivious to the fact that minority tribes have different appellations for the same realities.[20] It was thus argued that that the so-called 'lack of land' of the minorities should not 'stand in the way of the recognition of our paramount chiefs, as we the tribes have and live on our own land.'[21] It was clear, they argued, that 'the discrimination complained of has not been addressed', as 'The White Paper fails to make a constitutional commitment to the liberty and recognition of, and the development and preservation of the languages and cultures of the non-Tswana speaking tribes in the country, other than the ethnic Tswana.'

The petition additionally accused government of having betrayed its original intention to move from ethnicity to territory as a basis for representation, by yielding to Tswana pressure to maintain their tribal identities and to be represented by chiefs who assume office by virtue of birth. 'While the Tswana chiefs will participate on the basis of their birth right as chiefs of their tribes, the non-Tswana groups will be elected to the House as sub-chiefs, that is, of an inferior status. [...] Territoriality as a basis of representation is only applicable to the non-Tswana-speaking tribes [as] their dominant ethnicities remain unrecognised'.

---

[20] E.g. 'Chief': She in Bakalanga, Shikati in Bayei.
[21] See the Midweek Sun, May 22, 2002, pp.2-3, "Minorities' Petition President Mogae'.

Finally it was argued that the proposed proceedings were undemocratic, because it was foreseen that that government employees should elect subchiefs and chiefs. It was said that the suggested changes were aimed at 'taking away people's rights to participate in the selection of those who should represent them in the House of Chiefs'. In the same manner it was pointed out that representation of the people would be asymmetrical, because - while it would be possible for homogenous Tswana speaking regions to have more than one paramount chief (e.g. Balete and Batlokwa for the southeast district, and Barolong and Bangwaketse for the southern district) - this would not possible for other regions shared by Tswana and other tribes (e.g. Tawana and Bayei of the northwest district).

Other voices critical of the revised white paper claimed it had left unresolved the fundamental issue of tribal inequality, and had actually brought things 'back to square one'. The ruling Botswana Democratic party and government had demonstrated that they supported the interests of the eight principal tribes and chosen few, making it difficult for the minority tribes to 'trust a government like this one'.[22]

What is important in the above case of minority tribes is the fact that these groups see paramount chieftaincy as a solution to their marginalisation. Through paramount chieftaincy they believe they could have the recognition and representation they seek as citizens of modern Botswana with a given cultural heritage. In other words, while they appreciate their political rights as individual citizens in modern Botswana, they lament their perceived collective subjection to Tswana culture. Hence the clamour for paramount chiefs of their own, and the refusal to endorse the

---

[22] See Mmegi, May 24, 2002, p. 20, 'Politicians Criticise Mogae'.

argument that chieftaincy is an outmoded institution in a modern context of rights.

Chapter 4

Conclusion

In this study, I have argued that, instead of being pushed aside by the modern power elites - as was widely predicted both by modernisation theorists and their critics - chieftaincy has displayed remarkable dynamics and adaptability to new socio-economic and political developments, without becoming totally transformed in the process. Chiefdoms and chiefs have become active agents in the quest by the new elites for ethnic, cultural symbols as a way of maximising opportunities at the centre of bureaucratic and state power, and at the home village where control over land and labour often require both financial and symbolic capital. Chieftaincy, in other words, remains central to ongoing efforts at developing democracy and accountability in line with the expectations of Africans as individual 'citizens' and also as 'subjects' of various cultural communities.

The ethnographic accounts on Cameroon and Botswana have provided evidence to challenge perspectives that present chiefs and chieftaincy as fundamentally undemocratic and that as an institution are trapped in tradition as a frozen reality. The notion that chieftaincy and chiefs are either compressors of individual rights with infinite might, or helpless zombies co-optable by custom or by the modern state, denies them of collective and individual agency. The empirical reality of actual chiefdoms and chiefs in Cameroon and Botswana suggests that these are, and have always been active agents even in the face of the most overwhelming structures of repression. For those who care to listen, chiefdoms and chiefs have sought to demonstrate that no situation can be too repressive for human agency, just as no agency can be so complete as to preclude hierarchies imposed by structures. Chieftaincy is a dynamic institution, constantly re-inventing itself to accommodate and be accommodated by new exigencies, and has proved phenomenal in its ability to seek conviviality between competing and often conflicting influences. Our scholarship should seek to capture the interplay between structure and agency that this suggests, rather than insisting on either structure or agency (Comaroff 1978; van Binsbergen 2003a:33-39; Comaroff and Comaroff 2009:98-116; Angwafo III 2009; Knierzinger 2011; Cook & Hardin 2013).

In the realm of democracy and accountability, chieftaincy in Africa has both influenced and been influenced by modern state institutions and liberalism. The result of this intercourse is a victory neither for 'tradition' nor for 'modernity', neither for 'chieftaincy' nor for 'liberal' democracy', neither for imported nor for indigenous rituals of verification and accountability, neither for 'might' nor for 'right', but a richer reality produced and shaped by both. Like democracy, chieftaincy may be subjected to the whims and caprices of the power elite, but such impulses are not frozen in time and space, nor are the elite a homogenous and immutable entity. Changing political and material realities determine what claims are made on chieftaincy, by whom and with what implications for democracy. The adaptability and continuous appeal of chieftaincy makes of accountability in Africa an unending project, an aspiration that is subject to renegotiation with changing circumstances and growing claims by individuals and communities for recognition and representation. How relevant we are as social scientists to this project depends on how accountable to Africa and Africans we are in our scholarship.

References

Ahidjo, A. 1964. *Contribution to national construction*. Paris: Présence Africaine.

Ajaegbo, D.I. 2014. "African Democratic Heritage: A Historical Case Study of the Igbo of Nigeria." *IOSR Journal of Humanities and Social Science (IOSR-JHSS)*, 19(4), 17-23.

Aka, E.A. 1984. "Some vital information about fo Angwafo III." In: *Focus on Nükwi Nü Fo Ndefru III: Mankon Cultural Festival 23-31 December 1984*. Eds. Eballa, Y. & Aka, E.A. Yaounde: SOPECAM [Société de Presse et d'Editions du Cameroun], 63-68.

Anamzoya, A.S. 2014. "Neither fish nor fowl": an analysis of status ambiguity of the Houses of Chiefs in Ghana." *The Journal of Legal Pluralism and Unofficial Law*, 46(2), 218-234.

Angwafo III, F. S.A.N. 2009. *Royalty and Politics: The Story of My Life*. Bamenda: Langaa.

Bank, L. and Southall, R. 1996. "Traditional Leaders in South Africa's New Democracy." *Journal of Legal Pluralism*, Vol. 37(38), 407-430.

Bauer, G. 2014. "What is wrong with a woman being chief?" Women Chiefs and Symbolic and Substantive." *Journal of Asian and African Studies*, DOI: 10.1177/0021909614545700, 1-16.

Bayart, J.-F. 1985. *L'Etat au Cameroun*. Paris: Presse de la Fondation Nationale des Sciences Politiques.

Beall, J. 2005. "Decentralizing Government and Decentering Gender: Lessons from Local Government Reform in South Africa." *Politics & Society*, 33(2), 253-276.

Beall, J. 2006. "Cultural Weapons: Traditions, Inventions and the Transition to Democratic Governance in Metropolitan Durban." *Urban Studies*, 43(2), 457–473.

Beall, J. Mkhize, S. and Vawda, S. 2005. "Emergent Democracy and 'Resurgent' Tradition: Institutions, Chieftaincy and Transition in KwaZulu-Natal." *Journal of Southern African Studies*, 31(4), 755-771.

Boafo-Arthur, K. 2001. "Chieftaincy and Politics in Ghana Since 1982." *West Africa Review*, 3, 1.

Buur, L. and Kyed, H.M. 2005. *State Recognition of Traditional Authority in Mozambique: The Nexus of Community Representation and State Assistance*. Uppsala: Nordiska Afrikainstitutet.

Cantwell, L. 2015. "Chiefly Power in a Frontline State: Kgosi Linchwe II, the Bakgatla and Botswana in the South African Liberation Struggle, 1948-1994." *Journal of Southern African Studies*, 41(2), 255-272.

Chabal, P. Feinman, G. and Skalnik, P. 2004. "Beyond States and Empires: Chiefdoms and Informal Politics." *Social Evolution & History*, 3(1), 22–40.

Chakunda, V. and Chikerema A.F. 2014. "Indeginisation of Democracy: Harnessing Traditional Leadership in Promoting Democratic Values in Zimbabwe." *Journal of Power, Politics & Governance*, 2(1), 67-78.

Cheka, C. 2008. "Traditional Authority at the Crossroads of Governance in Republican Cameroon." *Africa Development*, XXXIII(2), 67–89.

Chigudu, D. 2015. "Assessing Policy Initiatives on Traditional Leadership to Promote Electoral Democracy in Southern Africa." *Mediterranean Journal of Social Sciences*, 6(1), 120-126.

Comaroff, J.L. 1978. "Rules and rulers: Political processes in a Tswana chiefdom." *Man*, 13, 1-20.

Comaroff, J.L. 1981. "The management of marriage in a Tswana chiefdom." In: *Essays on African Marriage in Southern Africa*. Eds. Krige, E.J. & Comaroff, J.L. Cape Town/Johannesburg: Juta & Co, 29-49.

Comaroff, J. and Comaroff, J. 1997. *Of Revelation and Revolution: The Dialectics of Modernity on a South African Frontier* (Volume Two). Chicago: Chicago University Press.

Comaroff J. and Comaroff J. 2009. *Ethnicity, Inc.* Scottsville: University of KwaZulu Natal Press.

Cook, S. and Hardin, R. 2013. "Performing Royalty in Contemporary Africa." *Cultural Anthropology*, 28(2), 227–251.

Dean, E. 2013. "The backbone of the village": gender, development, and traditional authority in rural Zanzibar." *Journal of Contemporary African Studies*, 31(1), 18-36.

De Vries, J. 1998. *Catholic mission, colonial government and indigenous response in Kom Cameroon*. Leiden: ASC Research Report 56.

Dingake, O.K. 1995. *Administrative law in Botswana: Cases, materials and commentaries*. Gaborone: University of Botswana.

Durham, D. 2002. "Uncertain citizens: Herero and the new intercalary subject in postcolonial Botswana." In: *Postcolonial Subjectivities in Africa*. Ed. Werbner, R. London, Zed, 139-170.

Eyoh, D. 1998. "Through the prism of a local tragedy: Political liberalisation, regionalism and elite struggles for power in Cameroon." *Africa*, 683, 338-359.

Fanthorpe, R. 2005. "On the Limits of Liberal Peace: Chiefs and Democratic Decentralization in Post-War Sierra Leone." *African Affairs*, 105(418), 27–49.

Ferguson, J. 1999. *Expectations of modernity: Myths and meanings of urban life on the Zambian copperbelt*. Berkeley: University of California Press.

Fisiy, F. C. 1995. "Chieftaincy in the modern state: An institution at the crossroads of democratic change." *Paideuma*, 41, 49-62.

Fisiy, F.C., & Goheen, M. 1998. "Power and the quest for recognition: Neo-traditional titles among the new elite in Nso, Cameroon." *Africa*, 683: 383-402.

Fokwang, J. 2003. *Chiefs and Democratic Transistion in Africa: An Ethnographic Study in the Chiefdoms of Tshivhase and Bali*. MA thesis. University of Pretoria.

Fokwang, J. 2009. *Mediating Legitimacy: Chieftaincy and Democratisation in Two African Chiefdoms*. Bamenda: Langaa.

Gardinier, D.E. 1963. *Cameroon: United Nations challenge to French policy*. Oxford: Oxford University Press.

Geschiere, P. 1993. "Chiefs and colonial rule in Cameroon: Inventing chieftaincy, French and British style." *Africa*, Vol. 63(2), 151-75.

Geschiere, P. & Gugler, J. (eds). 1998. "The politics of primary patriotism." *Africa*, 683, 309-319.

Geschiere, P. & Nyamnjoh, F. 1998. "Witchcraft as an issue in the "politics of belonging": Democratization and urban migrants' involvement with the home village." *African Studies Review*, Vol. 41, 69-92.

Geschiere, P. & Nyamnjoh, F. 2000. "Capitalism and autochthony: The seesaw of mobility and belonging." *Public Culture*, 12, 423-452.

Goheen, M. 1992. "Chiefs, sub-chiefs and local control: Negotiations over land, struggles over meaning." *Africa*, 623, 389-412.

Gonçalves, E. 2002. *Perceptions of Traditional Authority in Southern Mozambique, 1992-2002: A Case Study in Mocumbi District, Inhambane.* BA Hons. Dissertation, University of Cape Town.

Goodfellow, T. & Lindemann, S. 2013. "The clash of institutions: traditional authority, conflict and the failure of "hybridity" in Buganda." *Commonwealth & Comparative Politics*, 51(1), 3-26.

Harneit-Sievers, A. 1998. "Igbo "Traditional rulers": Chieftaincy and the state in Southeastern Nigeria." *Afrika Spectrum*, 33, 57-79.

Harrison, G. 2002. "Traditional Power and its Absence in Mecúfi, Mozambique." *Journal of Contemporary African Studies*, 20, 107-130.

Hendricks, F. and Ntsebeza, L. 1999. "Chiefs and Rural Local Government in Post-apartheid South Africa." *African Journal of Political Science*, Vol.4(1), 99-126.

Jua, N.B. 1995. "Indirect Rule in Colonial and Postcolonial Cameroon." *Paideuma* (41), 39-47.

Kelly, J.E. 2015. "Bantu Authorities and Betterment in Natal: The Ambiguous Responses of Chiefs and Regents, 1955–1970." *Journal of Southern African Studies*, 41(2), 273-297.

Kelsall, T. 2003. "Rituals of Verification: Indigenous and Imported Accountability in Northern Tanzania." *Africa*, Vol.73(2), 174-201.

King, B. H. 2005. "Spaces of Change: Tribal Authorities in the Former KaNgwane Homeland, South Africa." *Area*, 37(1), 64-72.

Knierzinger, J. 2011. *Chieftaincy and Development in Ghana: From Political Intermediaries to Neotraditional Development Brokers.* Working Papers of the Department of Anthropology and African Studies of the Johannes Gutenberg University Mainz, No. 124.

Kompi, B. and Twala, C. 2014. "The African National Congress and Traditional Leadership in a Democratic South Africa: Resurgence or Revival in the Era of Democratisation?" *Anthropologist*, 17(3), 981-989.

Konings, P. 1996. "Chieftaincy, labour control and capitalist development in Cameroon." *Journal of Legal Pluralism and Unofficial Law*, 37-38, 329-346.

Konings, P. 1999. "The "Anglophone problem" and chieftaincy in Anglophone Cameroon." In: *African chieftaincy in a new socio-political landscape.* Eds. van Rouveroy van Nieuwaal, E.A.B., & van Dijk, R. Hamburg/Münster, LIT Verlag, 181-206.

Konings, P. 2003. "Chieftaincy and Privatisation in Anglophone Cameroon." In: *The Dynamics of Power and the Rule of Law: Essays on Africa and Beyond.* Ed. van Binsbergen, W. Munster: African Studies Centre Leiden/Lit Verlag, 79-99.

Konings, P. 2009. *Neoliberal Bandwagonism: Civil society and the politics of belonging in Anglophone Cameroon.* Bamenda: Langaa.

Koter, D. 2013. "King makers: Local Leaders and Ethnic Politics in Africa." *World Politics* 65(2), 187–232.

Le Vine, V.T. 1964. *The Cameroons: From mandate to independence.* Berkeley: University of California Press.

Linchwe II, K.K. 1989. "The role a chief can play in Botswana's democracy." In: *Democracy in Botswana.* Eds.

Holm, J., & Molutsi, P. Gaborone: Macmillan Botswana, 99-102.

LiPuma, E. and Koelble, T.A. 2009. "Deliberative democracy and the politics of traditional leadership in South Africa: A case of despotic domination or democratic deliberation?" *Journal of Contemporary African Studies*, 27(2), 201-223.

Lloyd, P.C. 1965. "The political structure of African kingdoms: An exploratory model." In: *Political systems and the distribution of power*. Ed. Michael P. Banton. London: Tavistock Publications, 63-112.

Logan, C. 2009. "Selected chiefs, elected councillors and hybrid democrats: popular perspectives on the co-existence of democracy and traditional authority." *Journal of Modern African Studies*, 47(1), 101–128.

Logan, C. 2013. "The Roots of Resilience: Exploring Popular Support for African Traditional Authorities." *African Affairs*, 112(448), 353–376.

Machacek, M. J. 2013. *New Institutionalisms and the Resurgence of Traditional Authority in Sub-Saharan Africa: the Buganda Case Study*. MA thesis, Calgary University, Alberta, Canada.

Magubane, Z. 2004. *Bringing the Empire Home: Race, Class, and Gender in Britain and Colonial South Africa*. Chicago: The University of Chicago Press.

Makahamadze, T., Grand, N. and. Tavuyanago, B. 2009. "The Role of Traditional Leaders in Fostering Democracy, Justice and Human Rights in Zimbabwe." *The African Anthropologist*, 16(1&2), 33-47

Makgala, C. J. 1999. *The introduction of the policy of indirect rule into Bechuanaland protectorate, 1926-43*. M. Phil, Research Dissertation, University of Cambridge.

Maloka, T.E. 1995. "Traditional Leaders and the Current Transition." *The African Communist*, 2nd Quarter, 35-43.

Maloka, T.E. 1996. "Populism and the Politics of Chieftaincy and Nation-building in the New South Africa." *Journal of Contemporary African Studies*, vol.14(2), 173-196.

Mamdani, M. 1996. *Citizen and subject: Contemporary Africa and the legacy of late colonialism*. Cape Town: David Philip.

Manson, A. 2013. "Mining and "Traditional Communities" in South Africa's "Platinum Belt": Contestations over Land, Leadership and Assets in North-West Province c.1996–2012." *Journal of Southern African Studies*, 39(2), 409-423.

Mappa, S. 1998. *Pouvoirs traditionnels et pouvoir d'etat en Afrique: L'illusion universaliste*. Paris: Karthala.

Matemba, Y.H. 2005. "A Chief Called "Woman": Historical Perspectives on the Changing Face of Bogosi (Chietainship) in Botswana, 1984-2004." *Jenda: A Journal of Culture and African Women Studies*, Issue 7, 1-22.

Mawere, M and Mayekiso, A. 2014. "Traditional Leadership, Democracy and Social Equality in Africa: The Role of Traditional Leadership in Emboldening Social Equality in South Africa." *International Journal of Politics and Good Governance*, 5(5.3), 1-11.

Mazibuko, S. 2014. "Rural Governance in South Africa: Is there a Place for Neo-Feudalism in a Democracy?" *Mediterranean Journal of Social Sciences*, 5(20), 2455- 2461.

Mazonde, I. (ed.) 2002. *Minorities in the millennium: Perspectives from Botswana*. Gaborone: Lightbooks.

Mbembe, A. 2001. *On the postcolony*. Berkeley: University of California Press.

Mercer, C. Page, B. & Evans, M. 2009. *Development and the African Diaspora: Place and the Politics of Home*. London: Zed Books.

Miaffo, D. 1993. *Chefferie traditionnelle et démocratie: Réflexion sur le destin du chef en régime pluraliste*. Douala: Editions Laakam.

Miaffo, D. & Warnier, J.-P. 1993. "Accumulation et ethos de la notabilité chez les Bamiléké." In: *Pathways to accumulation in Cameroon*. Eds. Geschiere, P. & Konings, P. Paris: Karthala, 33-69.

Molomo, M. (ed.) 2000. *Pula: Elections and Democracy in Botswana*, 14(1).

Moore, H.L., and Sanders, T. 2001. "Magical Interpretations and Material Realities: An Introduction." In: *Magical Interpretations, Material Realities: Modernity, Witchcraft and the Occult in Postcolonial Africa*. Eds. Moore, H.L., & Sanders, T. London: Routledge, 1-27.

Mope Simo, J.A. 1997. "Land Disputes and the Impact on Disintegration in Contemporary Western Grassfields: Case Study of the Ndop Plain Chiefdoms." In: *Regional balance and national integration in Cameroon: Lessons learned and the uncertain future*. Eds. Nkwi, P.N., & Nyamnjoh, F.B. Yaounde: ASC/ICASSRT[ASC stands for African Studies Centre Leiden, and ICASSRT a local research institute in Yaounde. This publication was a collaborative effort by the two], 225-241.

Morapedi, W.G. 2010. "Demise or Resilience? Customary Law and Chieftaincy in Twenty-First Century Botswana." *Journal of Contemporary African Studies*, 28(2), 215-230.

Morton, F. and Ramsay, J. (eds.) 1987. *The Birth of Botswana: A History of the Bechuanaland Protectorate from 1910 to 1966*. Gaborone: Longman Botswana.

Moseki, A. 2003. "Chieftainship, Legitimacy and Succession in Tswana States: The Case of Bakwena, 1930 to Present." *SOC 422 Project Report*, University of Botswana.

Mouiche, I. 1992. *Les autorités traditionnelles dans la vie politique moderne au Cameroun: Le cas de l'organisation municipale du Noun.* Unpublished thesis. University of Yaoundé.

Mouiche, I. 1997. "Le royaume bamoun, les chefferies Bamiléké et l'etat au Cameroun." In: *Regional balance and national integration in Cameroon: lessons learned and the uncertain future.* Eds. Nkwi, P.N., & Nyamnjoh, F.B. Yaounde: ASC/ICASSRT, 306-322.

Murray, A. 1990. *Peoples' Rights: The Case of BaYei Separatism.* Maseru: National University of Lesotho, Human and Peoples' Rights Project Monograph No.9.

Ngomba, T., 2012, *Political Campaign Communication in Sub-Saharan Africa: The Cameroonian Experience in a Global Perspective*, PhD Thesis in Media and Communication Studies, Aarhus University, Denmark.

Ngwenya, B. N. 2000. *Gender and social transformation through burial societies in a contemporary Southern African society: The case of Botswana.* Ph.D. dissertation. Michigan State University.

Nkwi, P.N. 1976. *Traditional government and social change: A study of the political institutions among the Kom of the Cameroon Grassfields.* Fribourg: University Press.

Nkwi, P.N. 1979. "Cameroon Grassfield chiefs and modern politics." *Paideuma*, 25, 99-115.

Nkwi, P.N., & Warnier, J.-P. 1982. *Elements for a history of the Western Grassfields.* Yaounde: University of Yaounde.

Ntsebeza, L. 1998. "Rural Local Government in Post-apartheid South Africa." *African Sociological Review*, 2(1), 153-164.

Ntsebeza, L. 2005. *Democracy compromised: Chiefs and the politics of the land in South Africa.* Leiden: Brill

Nyamnjoh, F.B. 1985. *Change in the concept of power amongst the Bum*, Master's thesis. F.L.S.H. [Faculté des Lettres et Sciences Humaines], Yaounde, Mimeo.

Nyamnjoh, F.B. 1999. "Cameroon: A country united by ethnic ambition and difference." *African Affairs*, 98, 101-118.

Nyamnjoh, F.B. 2001a. "Delusions of Development and the Enrichment of Witchcraft Discourses in Cameroon." In: *Magical Interpretations, Material Realities: Modernity, Witchcraft and the Occult in Postcolonial Africa*. Eds. Henrietta L. Moore and Todd Sanders. London: Routledge, 28-49.

Nyamnjoh, F.B. 2001b. "Review article: Expectations of modernity in Africa or a future in the rear-view mirror?" *Journal of Southern African Studies*, 272, 363-369.

Nyamnjoh, F.B. 2002a. "A child is one person's only in the womb": Domestication, agency and subjectivity in the Cameroonian Grassfields." In: *Postcolonial subjectivities in Africa*. Ed. Werbner, R. London: Zed, 111-138.

Nyamnjoh, F.B. 2002b. "Local attitudes towards citizenship and foreigners in Botswana: An appraisal of recent press stories." *Journal of Southern African Studies*, 28, 755-776.

Nyamnjoh, F.B. 2005. *Africa's Media, Democracy and the Politics of Belonging*. London: Zed Books.

Nyamnjoh, F.B. 2012. "Blinded by Sight: Diving the Future of Anthropology in Africa." *Africa Spectrum* 47(2-3), 63-92.

Nyamnjoh, F.B. 2013. "Politics of Back-Scratching in Cameroon and Beyond." In: *Non-Western Reflection on Politics*. Eds. Petr Drulák and Šárka Moravcová. Frankfurt am Main: Peter Lang, 35-53.

Nyamnjoh, F.B. & Rowlands, M. 1998. "Elite Associations and the Politics of Belonging in Cameroon." *Africa* 68(3), 320-337.

O'Laughlin, B. 2000. "Class and the customary: The ambiguous legacy of the indigenato in Mozambique." *African Affairs*, 99, 5-42.

Omagu, D.O. 2013. "African Culture and Tradition at the Crossroad: The Institution of Chieftaincy and the Paradox of Modernity in Bekwarra." *Canadian Social Science*, 9(6), 1-14.

Oomen, B. 2000a. "We must now go back to our history": Retraditionalisation in a Northern Province Chieftaincy." *African Studies*, 59, 71-95.

Oomen, B. 2000b. *Tradition on the Move: Chiefs, Democracy and Change in Rural South Africa.* (NiZA-Cahier 6) Amsterdam: NiZA.

Oomen, B. 2003. "Legal Syncretism in Sekhukhune: Local Law and the Power of Traditional Leaders in Northern South Africa." In: *The Dynamics of Power and the Rule of Law: Essays on Africa and Beyond.* Ed. van Binsbergen, W. Munster: African Studies Centre Leiden/Lit Verlag, 167-193.

Orock, R.T.E. 2014. "Welcoming the "Fon Of Fons": Anglophone Elites and the Politics of Hosting Cameroon's Head of State." *Africa*, 84 (2), 226-245.

Owusu-Mensah, I. 2014. "Politics, Chieftaincy and Customary Law in Ghana's Fourth Republic." *The Journal of Pan African Studies*, 6(7), 261-278.

Parsons, N., Henderson, W., & Tlou, T. 1995. *Seretse Khama: 1921-1980.* Gaborone: The Botswana Society.

Peter, I., 2014. "Reconsidering Place of Traditional Institutions under the Nigerian Constitution: A Comparative Analysis." *Journal of Law, Policy and Globalization*, 31, 135-148.

Republic of Botswana. 2000. *Report of the presidential commission of inquiry into sections 77, 78 and 79 of the constitution of Botswana*. Gaborone: Government Printer.

Ribot, J.C. 1999. "Decentralisation, participation and accountability in Sahelian forestry: Legal instruments of political-administrative control." *Africa*, 691, 23-66.

Rowlands, M., & Warnier, J.-P. 1988. "Sorcery, power and the modern state in Cameroon." *Man*, 231, 118-32.

Schapera, I. 1938. *A handbook of Tswana law and custom: Compiled for the Bechuanaland protectorate administration*. Hamburg/Münster: LIT Verlag.

Schipper, W.J.J., 1990. "Homo Caudatus: Imagination and Power in the Field of Literature." In: *White and Black: Imagination and Cultural Confrontation (Bulletin 320)*. Schipper, W.J.J., Idema, W.L., and Leyten, H.M. Amsterdam: Royal Tropical Institute – Amsterdam, 11-30.

Selolwane, O.D. 2000. *Botswana: The challenges of consolidating good governance and plural politics*. Paper presented at the Workshop on promoting good governance and wider civil society participation in Eastern and Southern Africa, Addis Ababa, 6-8 November 2000.

Selolwane, O.D. 2002. "Monopoly politikos: How Botswana's opposition parties have helped sustain one-party dominance." *African Sociological Review*, 6, 68-90.

Solway, J. 2002. "Navigating the "neutral" state: "Minority" rights in Botswana." *Journal of Southern African Studies*, 28, 711-730.

Tabapssi, F.T. 1999. *Le modèle migratoire Bamiléké Cameroun et sa crise actuelle: Perspectives économique et culturelle*. Leiden: University of Leiden.

Turner, R.L. 2014. "Traditional, Democratic, Accountable? Navigating Citizen-Subjection in Rural South Africa." *Africa Spectrum*, 49(1), 27-54.

Ubink, J. 2007. "Traditional Authority Revisited: Popular Perceptions of Chiefs and Chieftaincy in Peri-Urban Kumasi, Ghana." *The Journal of Legal Pluralism and Unofficial Law*, 39(55), 123-161.

Uwalaka, E. 2014. "An Empirical Investigation of Attitudes and Beliefs toward the Resurgence of Traditional Titles and Honors among the Igbos." *International Journal of Humanities and Social Science*, 4(13), 22-29.

Valsecchi, P. 2007. *"He who sets the boundary". Chieftaincy as a "necessary" institution in modern Ghana.* Department of Communication, Working Paper No. 3, University of Teramo.

van Binsbergen, W. 2003a. "Introduction: The Dynamics of Power and the Rule of Law in Africa and Beyond: Theoretical Perspectives on Chiefs, the State, Agency, Customary Law, and Violence." In: *The Dynamics of Power and the Rule of Law: Essays on Africa and Beyond.* Ed. van Binsbergen, W. Munster: African Studies Centre Leiden/Lit Verlag, 9-47.

van Binsbergen, W. (ed.). 2003b. *The Dynamics of Power and the Rule of Law: Essays on Africa and Beyond.* Munster: African Studies Centre Leiden/Lit Verlag.

van Kessel, I., and Oomen, B. 1997. "One Chief, One Vote": The Revival of Traditional Authorities in Post-apartheid South Africa." *African Affairs*, vol. 96, 561-585.

van Rouveroy van Nieuwaal, E.A.B, & van Dijk, R. (eds). 1999. *African chieftaincy in a new socio-political landscape.* Hamburg/Münster: LIT Verlag.

van Rouveroy van Nieuwaal, E.A.B. 2000. *L'état en Afrique face à la chefferie: Le cas du Togo*. Paris: ASC-Karthala.

Warnier, J.-P. 1993. "The king as a container in the Cameroon Grassfields." *Paideuma*, 39, 303-319.

Warnier, J-P. 2007. *The Pot-King: The Body and Technologies of Power*. Leiden, The Netherlands: Brill.

Waterman, C.A. 1997. "Our Tradition is a Very Modern Tradition: Popular Music & the Construction of Pan-Yoruba Identity." In: *Readings in African Popular Culture*. Ed. Barber, K. Oxford: James Currey, 48-53.

Werbner, R. 2002a. "Cosmopolitan Ethnicity, Entrepreneurship and the Nation: Minority Elites in Botswana." *Journal of Southern African Studies*, Vol.28(4), 632-753.

Werbner, R. 2002b. "Conclusion: Citizenship and the Politics of Recognition in Botswana." In: *Minorities in the Millennium: Perspectives from Botswana*. Ed. Mazonde, I. Gaborone: Lightbooks, 117-135.

Werbner, R. 2002c. "Introduction: Challenging Minorities, Difference and Tribal Citizenship in Botswana." *Journal of Southern African Studies*, Vol.28(4), 671-684.

Werbner, R. and Gaitskell, D. (Guest-eds). 2002. "Minorities and Citizenship in Botswana." *Journal of Southern African Studies*, Vol.28(4).

West, H.G., and Kloeck-Jenson, S. 1999. "Betwixt and Between: "Traditional Authority" and Democratic Decentralization Post-war Mozambique." *African Affairs*, Vol. 98, 455-484.

Williams, J.M. 2004. "Leading from behind: Democratic consolidation and the chieftaincy in South Africa." *Journal of Modern African Studies*, 42(1), 113-136.

Williams, J.M. 2009. "Legislating "Tradition" in South Africa." *Journal of Southern African Studies*, 35(1), 191-209.

Printed in the United States
By Bookmasters